Opportunity
ROCKS!™

Be a Rock Star in
Business and Beyond

5-19-23
Eric,
Yeu Killed it
ReelOn!

Marvelless Mark Kamp

Opportunity Rocks is a registered trademark of Millennia
Productions, Inc.

For information about special discounts on bulk purchases,
please contact Marvelless Mark
at 1-877-9ROCKON (1-877-976-2566)
or rockstar@marvellessmark.com

www.marvellessmark.com

Library of Congress Cataloging-in-Publication Data is available.

ISBN-13: 978-1-792-72918-8

This book is dedicated to my first real band, my family. My father and mother who were the President and CEO's, or the drummers. They set the beat that I still follow to this day. They taught me that practice makes perfect.

I also want to acknowledge the other members of my original band. My sister was like the bass player. She provided the structure and backbone for our family song, but like most bass-players, never got a lot of credit for it. And my brother was like the rhythm guitarist—making the music complete while standing back and enabling me to take the front man position.

Table of Contents

Chapter 4

Chapter 5

Chapter 6

Chapter 7

Chapter 8

Chapter 9

Chapter 10

Chapter 11

Chapter 12

Chapter 13

Resources

Acknowledgements

Heartfelt thanks to KGB for bringing this goal and vision to reality in a smooth and professional manner. You're truly a gifted and wonderful soul. Thanks for rockin' it!

To DW for his scripting, research and belief in the Opportunity Rocks keynote and motivational speech that ignited the idea for this book. And to my POTM friend for his encouragement to take the first step. I know it's only rock and roll, but I like it!

And a couple of rock star shout outs to The Ol' Auction Man and Barbie in Heaven, DS in Chicago, Dodo for the next level, TSP, The Mixx, KAG, Mr. Rocket, Boogie, Turntable Wizard, AP, Twisted Tim, The Scozz, The Candy Man, Willy K, and MW. You all rock! And all of you gave me opportunities *to* rock!

To so many others way too many to mention—thanks for the ideas, referrals, bookings, encouragement, support, discoveries and sometimes just showing up! But my greatest thanks goes to my many fans, supporters and friends who have fueled my rock star journey. My promise to you—the best is yet to come!

Foreword

Rock 'n' Roll is a business. A lot of peace-and-love type songwriters will tell you that's not true, but don't let them fool you. You don't eat, you can't play. Talent is important, but it won't get you where you want to go all by itself. If you want to be a professional, then get serious about music as a profession. The musicians that make it long enough to become rock stars, the ones who stick around through the years, are the ones who know that. Rock stars aren't just killer musicians, they're entrepreneurs too.

But listen, that doesn't mean that music isn't a lot of fun. It's awesome. You get to see the world. You get paid to do what you love. People buy you beer. Oh, and the screaming girls. Yeah, that's pretty cool, too. You can be serious about living your dream, about success, and still have a blast. You can do it without selling your soul. You just can't do it without selling your music. You have to have a vision, an attitude, and a high tolerance for failure. But if you can be bulletproof and persistent, you might get to be a star.

That's what *Opportunity Rocks* is about. This book is for everyone who has wanted to be a rock star at what they do. You don't have to be a guitar god for the message to apply to you. It's about helping you achieve your potential—and get the gold records—no matter what kind of life you lead.

Everybody needs to learn what rock stars know. Marvelless Mark has broken it down for you, the things you need to start doing in order to rock your own life. What's keeping you from pursuing your career like you were chasing a hit single? Why shouldn't you think of your family as a band? That sounds way cooler than trying to live like business is a battlefield, or like you're some modern day Machiavelli, or like someone moved your...well, you get the idea. Mark's point is that you can be ambitious, set goals, go after the things you want, without turning into a stuffed shirt.

This book is full of practical ideas, and examples of legendary musicians who made them work. Mark's here to tell you that you can pursue your own vision, make decisions and handle change, and stay in it for the long haul. And if you can do those things, you can be a rock star, too...of the boardroom, the softball field, or the courtroom. That's up to you.

Opportunity Rocks!
Be a Rock Star in
Business and Beyond

I'll bet nobody has to tell you what a rock star is. Say the word and your thoughts go immediately to your favorite band or solo artist—to bright lights, blistering guitar chords, screaming girls, and wildly tossing hair. Maybe you picture Mick Jagger strutting across a stage, or Steven Tyler howling into the mic. Maybe you think of Lady GaGa's glittering costumes, Natalie Merchant's smooth vocals. No matter the musician you envision, the point is, you know who they are and what they represent—talent, success, respect, and the really good tables at trendy restaurants.

Think about it—the word "rock star" has become a metaphor for the same reason. A rock star can be anyone in any industry who has earned fame, admiration, and success by being the best at what they do. That's what this book is about: helping **you** become the best at what you do and achieving rock star status in your career and your life.

Rock 'n' roll legends have a lot to teach us, and not just about how to trash a hotel room. Music is a business. Most truly successful musicians understand that you have to treat it like a business and find a way to keep your passion for the music at the same time. The artists who excel at this become rock stars.

The rock legends, the icons, the geniuses of music all have a story. They started out with little or nothing; they had challenges along the way. Each one had a never surrender, never give up attitude. These are the people who hung in there, no matter what, and eventually became the legends they are today.

You have more in common with them than you think. At some point, maybe when you were in school, you decided on the career path you wanted to take, and now you're on that journey. You face challenges and setbacks. But you have made it this far, and you can use your talents and determination to get further if you make smart choices and you don't give up. We can take the ideas and techniques of those legendary musicians and apply them to just about any field to help you become a rock star, too.

How do I know? My name is Mark Kamp—you can call me "Marvelless Mark." I acquired my radio and stage name in the '80s. I have branded myself this way because of my "less gives you more" attitude. (Also, it's easier to copyright and trademark a name when you misspell it.)

My own life has been a kind of rock odyssey. It has led me to a place where I can help people with the things I love most—music and motivation. I started out as a farm kid in Missouri, a place where kids learn to do everything from driving a tractor to castrating pigs, from mechanics to construction work. Our family knew firsthand that if you didn't have a solid work ethic, you had no crop and you didn't eat.

In high school, I started a DJ business with some friends in our small town. I loved the limelight and pushing the envelope (something my less visionary friends called "showing off"), and when I graduated, I found part time work at a local radio station. I worked two other full time jobs while learning the ropes of the entertainment business. I had a great radio mentor who taught me all about how to connect with people, and about how sales, marketing, programming, and managing people depend on understanding them. I kept the local DJ gig as a sideline, started to really study what some of my favorite rock legends did to create a public persona, and attended a lot of concerts. I applied what I learned to my show—adding costumes, special effects, props, interaction, video—I was constantly looking for ways to stand out, to be different and better than any of our competitors in the county or even the state. I was branding myself and didn't even know it.

I made the move to the big city and got a job doing promotions, DJing, and nightclub management. Around 1990, I relocated to Florida to pursue a career as a cruise ship entertainer and program director; but I never made it to sea. An entertainment producer discovered me performing at an event and connected me with an entertainment management company that helped me reinvent myself, hone and fine tune my talents, and sent me on the road as Marvelless Mark: The Ultimate Interactive Entertainment Experience for Corporate America. Soon, I was opening or closing for big name rock bands, comedians, and some of the greatest inspirational and motivational speakers. It was awesome. When I wasn't on stage, I was watching them and listening to everything they had to say about success, motivation, happiness, and turning your dreams to reality. It was a free education. With some creative guidance, I kept the show growing and eventually started my own show band.

That's what I was doing when the American economy hit the skids. In the aftermath of the initial crash, I realized how much people needed all of the information I had learned, and how much they still crave entertainment as part of learning, meetings, and events. So I was led to reinvent myself once again with a more edu-tainment (entertainment with a message) format. The whole country has faced many new challenges in the last decade, and I believe people need music, motivation, and inspiration. You can get education and have a good time at the same time.

My model for business is the Beatles. They were four guys who kept each others negative tendencies in check. They balanced each other and the total was greater than the sum parts. And that's how I see business. Great things in business are never done by one person, they are done by a team of people.

~ Steve Jobs, Apple Computers[1]

Thanks to what I have learned from all of my own personal rock stars—my parents, mentors, great fans, life style gurus, and business coaches like Steven Covey and Anthony Robbins, bands like KISS, and lessons from my own mistakes along the way, I have had a pretty rockin' life so far. I think anyone can. It all started on a farm...I was forced to be creative in order to entertain myself and others, to dream and to envision that someday I would travel the world as a rock star. I just didn't know at the time it would be as a <u>business</u> rock star. Now, I'm here to help you pursue your dreams and visions in the most fun, entertaining way possible.

Before we crank up the music and get to taking care of business (or as Elvis would say, TCB), let's make sure we're all in the same key. We'll start with the characteristics of a real rock star:

- superior talent
- confidence
- hard working

- determination
- high standards
- connection to audience
- able to inspire passionate loyalty

A rock star has natural gifts, sure; but, they also have other qualities that help them make the most of those gifts. To make the most of your talent, focus your energy, and go the distance, first you have to master some basic chords.

Mastering the Basic Chords

Most rock 'n' roll is built around a few guitar chords—the sounds that the instrument makes when multiple strings are struck at the same time. Put together a few simple chords and you can build a limitless variety of great songs. With that in mind, this book is built around these basic chords with a foundational concept connected to each one. Every rock band starts out by playing songs with three fundamental chords: F, B, and A. Consequently, most rock songs are built around these three simple chords. So that's where we'll start, too.

Section 1 – The Basic Chords

Chapters 1 - 3 describe the A chord; that's about Attitude.
Chapters 4 - 6 describe the B chord, and that's your Band.
Chapters 7 - 9 describe the F chord, and that's your Fans.

Just like our musician friends, once we get those down, we will master the rest of the chords, the ones that add color and depth to the music. These are C, D, G, and E.

Section 2 – Advanced Chords

Chapter 10 is the G chord, where we consider your Goals.

Chapter 11 is the D chord, where we talk about your Decisions.

Chapter 12 is the C chord, where we discuss Change.

Chapter 13 is the E chord, where we talk about Energy.

So enough of the pre-show. Let's get to the music. Just one last question… are you ready to ROCK?

Section 1 – The Basic Chords

A Chord
ATTITUDE

You do not merely want to be considered just the best of the best. You want to be considered the only ones who do what you do.

~ Jerry Garcia[2]

Be More than a One Hit Wonder

I bet you are familiar with the term "One Hit Wonder." It refers to a band or artist who has one hugely popular song, and then fades into obscurity. You might hear that song on the classic rock station for years, but somehow they never manage to hit the charts again. The first success is nice, for sure (and it's better than never having your 15 minutes of fame at all), but it certainly isn't what anyone dreams about doing with their lives or their gifts. Everyone wants to hit the charts again and again.

You don't want to be a One Hit Wonder in your life or career, either. Who wants to fizzle out after one early success and then spend the years wondering why they couldn't repeat it? So let's think for a moment about the difference between a One Hit Wonder and a genuine Rock Star.

1. Both have talent.
2. Both put effort and determination into reaching a certain goal.
3. Both attract attention for producing something—in this case, a song—that people appreciate.

The One Hit Wonder and the Rock Star got to that first level of success by doing the same thing: creating a song that everyone can identify with, and performing it well. The difference is that rock stars do this continually over time. That's how they develop the fan base that sustains them.

A One Hit Wonder can't sustain that effort. He doesn't keep that connection to audiences. He doesn't change or grow enough to stay fresh. A true rock star has momentum. She keeps high standards for her work and she pushes herself to keep growing. The key to building that momentum is our A chord. It's all about ATTITUDE.

Rock 'n' roll is an attitude; it's not a musical form of a strict sort. It's a way of doing things, of approaching things. Writing can be rock 'n' roll, or a movie can be rock 'n' roll. It's a way of living your life.

~ Lester Bangs[3]

Attitude, Like Rock, Is a Way of Life

Lester Bangs was a musician and writer who worked for *Rolling Stone Magazine*. Are you familiar with all glittering rock gods of the 1960s and 70s? He saw them strut and howl in their prime. He saw first-hand the confidence and self-assurance that it takes to work a crowd. But read that quotation again. "Attitude" for Lester Bangs is "a way of living your life." And in his philosophy, rock 'n' roll is a certain type of attitude. It's a mindset, a way of living your life. If you have the right attitude, it will manifest as a kind of confidence that you take with you on stage and into the world.

The way I see it, everything you need to know about a rock 'n' roll attitude comes down to three things: failure, opportunity, and yourself.

Chapter 1

Failure

I did this the way you are supposed to. I played every club in New York City and I bombed in every club and then killed it in every club and I found myself as an artist. I learned how to survive as an artist, get real, and how to fail, and then figure out who I was as singer and performer. And, I worked hard.

~Lady Gaga[4]

Musicians live in perpetual fear of bombing on stage. Over half of U.S. households have at least one member who can play a musical instrument, but only a small fraction ever perform in public.[5] It's a pretty scary thought... getting in front of a crowd, getting booed, getting bottles thrown at your head. No thanks! It's no surprise that so few people who can play an instrument will actually do so in front of strangers. According to research recently published in *Psychology Today*, the higher a person's fear of failure is, the more statistically likely they are to procrastinate and fail to take action.

Like everyone else, a rock star has to start out as an unknown. They have to take risks. They have to overcome the fear of failure in order to get out on that stage the first time and they have to find the courage to keep going out even if the worst happens. Would you boo Prince off the stage? Audiences did when he was an opening act for the Rolling Stones.

According to a Harvard business study, "failure is actually the norm" for most ventures. 70-80% don't see sufficient return on investments; 90-95% make projections that they subsequently don't meet; and 30-40% of start-ups fail entirely.[6] The lesson here is that every venture and every person experiences failure at some point. What matters is what you choose to do about it.

You build on failure. You use it as a stepping stone. Close the door on the past. You don't try to forget the mistakes, but you don't dwell on it. You don't let it have any of your energy, or any of your time, or any of your space.

~Johnny Cash[7]

OK, Johnny Cash isn't really a "rock" star. But he is a legend. And he was the Man in Black. You should listen to him because your attitude about failure actually has a lot of influence over your potential success.

If you become so discouraged that you quit pursuing your goals, you will certainly never reach them. But if you are able to observe your failures, make improvements, and try again, lots of good things happen. You improve your skills.

You discover new strategies. And, eventually, you find your fan base.

A Chord Drill

Write down one small thing that you wish you could to do at work or in public, something that would be good for you, but scares you too much to try. It could be as simple as "I wish I could tell my boss that my name isn't Shirley." Get a friend to help you practice an interaction where you do that thing in a positive and appropriate way. Set a deadline (e.g. "one week from today", "next time it happens", "next month"). After a few drills, make a commitment to do this thing, and "perform" your A chord in public.

We all fail somewhere along the line. The race you lost, the test you didn't pass and, in my case, the record execs who claimed "you'll never make it in the music business." Whatever. The point is, you get up, brush yourself off and get on with life. ... it is what you learn from your failure that makes all the difference.

~Jon Bon Jovi, Bon Jovi[8]

Don't be afraid of failure - embrace that too. Dare to fail. If you never fail, you've never taken risks, and that's no way to take on this life.

~Richie Sambora, Bon Jovi[9]

The band Bon Jovi was turned down by multiple record companies when they started playing in the early 1980s. But they kept promoting their songs aggressively and eventually convinced a local radio station to include one of their songs on a compilation. That single's success opened the door to the regional market and touring opportunities that allowed them to build a reputation and refine their sound. Four years later, they released *Slippery When Wet*, the album that went gold and made them the darlings of MTV. They did not let early failures defeat them; they exercised persistence and kept working on their craft in the meantime. When that door opened, they were ready.

What all of these rock stars have in common was that they held on to their dreams and their core values, even when they encountered obstacles. They stayed focused and worked hard; they didn't try to cheat or fake their way to the top. If you read the tabloids, you've heard that rock stars aren't always the nicest people. Some of them are cranky, self-indulgent, rude, whiny, or just plain weird. In other words, they're still *human*. But the ones who last, who survive their own excesses, are the ones who maintain a certain integrity and commitment to the quality of their work. They work through the failure and disappointment instead of trying to get around it.

The same Harvard business study I mentioned earlier describes a difference between "enterprise failure" and "personal failure."[10] Let me break this down: the distinction is not between setbacks in your career versus your personal life. What they mean is that there is a difference between failure that comes from circumstances or misjudgment and failure that comes from bad ethical choices. It is much harder to come back from a problem caused by lies, illegal activity, or morally questionable practices. I'm sure you'll be a real sweetheart even when you're rich and famous. Just remember that you can recover from just about any loss or setback easier than you can the loss of integrity.

If you stick to your integrity and your goals, eventually somebody will appreciate what you are doing on a wider scale.

~ Bonnie Raitt[11]

Makes me that much stronger
Makes me work a little bit harder
It makes me that much wiser
So thanks for making me a fighter
Made me learn a little bit faster
Made my skin a little bit thicker
Makes me that much smarter
So thanks for making me a fighter

~ Christina Aguilera, "Fighter"[12]

Let your failures educate you and feed your ambitions. Nurture the persistence, flexibility, and resilience in your character; everyone has a bit of those buried inside them. If you still need a little food for thought about failure, here's a tip from a rock star of the ice rink, hockey legend Wayne Gretzky: "You miss 100% of the shots you don't take."

Chapter 2

Opportunity

Our first chapter closed with a reminder that you're 100% guaranteed to miss when you don't shoot. That should be a strong motivator if you've ever read one. I'll put it another way: you might miss some opportunities when you reach for them, but you will miss all of them it you don't reach at all.

Once you have learned to push past fear, you will get better and better at learning to see and to seize opportunities. The rock 'n' roll attitude is all about seeing opportunity in everything: opportunity to learn and grow your skill set, opportunity to make connections with people who may join your band or become your fans. It will allow you to perceive events or circumstances as opportunities where others might see a threat.

Let's go back to the start of our A chord material, to the opening quotation from the Grateful Dead's Jerry Garcia. It takes confidence to make the claim that you want to be seen as the "only one who does what you do." It takes fearlessness, or at least the ability to push past your fear in order to try. More than that, it takes vision and imagination—a sense of the possibilities.

When the Grateful Dead were at the height of their popularity as a touring group, the music industry was terrified of bootleg recordings. Record executives, producers, and managers worried that their profits would disappear if anyone brought a recording device to a show. How did they respond? Security started frisking fans at the gates.

But the Grateful Dead had a different idea. They welcomed the cameras and recorders; they invited their fans to bring equipment and even set up a special section on the floor for people who brought recording gear. Not only did this create a bond with their fans (saying, in effect, "we trust you and we want to share with you"), but these recordings ended up being terrific networking and marketing tools. Fans would leave the show and play their recordings at parties and for friends, who liked what they heard and bought an album or came to the next show. The Dead were doing social media before social media was even invented!

Jack White of The White Stripes is also great at cultivating opportunity.[13] At the age of 29, he was already a popular guitarist and budding producer. But most of his production credits were for his own band. He had made the acquaintance of country legend Loretta Lynn, and while visiting her home, discovered that she had a stash of unrecorded songs. He proposed a collaboration. The result was *Van Lear Rose (2004)*, a crossover album between country and rock sounds. It won the 70-year-old Lynn her first Grammy and put White on the map as a producer. His label, Third Man Records, has since developed into an indie powerhouse known for its innovative music and entrepreneurial spirit.

Chapter 3

Yourself

When you follow your heart, you're never supposed to do things because of what you think people might say. You do it for the opposite reasons.

~ will.i.am[14]

Want to know what you have in common with every rock star that has ever lived? <u>You are your own best product</u>. You are the sum of your talent, your efforts, and your values. If you want to be comfortable and confident selling Brand You, then invest your energies into developing your inner rock star:

- *Practice your instrument.* Tap into your gifts and commit to using them well. Educate yourself. Practice. Strive for excellence.
- *Move people with your music.* Use your powers for good. Connect with the people around you. Encourage them. Use your unique skills to make a positive impact. Making money and making the world a better place are not mutually exclusive. Rock stars do it all the time.
- *Put your gold records on the wall.* If you have a success, celebrate! Tell the people you love. Put

those titles and mementos on your wall, your website, wherever. You won't have to point them out; others will notice on their own.

- *Look toward the next record.* Set goals for yourself. When you achieve them, set new ones. If a project fails or disappoints, prepare to try again. Never let your last album be your last album. And don't make the same record twice.

Bring Your Swagger

*I used to walk down the street like I was a f****** star... I want people to walk around delusional about how great they can be - and then to fight so hard for it every day that the lie becomes the truth.*

~ Lady Gaga[15]

If you're going to be a rock star, you've got to have swagger! Your posture, your voice, and your dress should be confident....probably a bit more confident than you actually feel. Behavioral research shows that people who display overconfidence actually succeed in multiple social situations more often than those who display ordinary or under-confidence.[16] Attitude should be part of your attitude. Does this mean you should act like a jerk, or be rude to everyone around you? Of course not; disrespect doesn't really breed loyalty or affection. But for better or worse, humans tend to make decisions based on appearance. If you look and sound like you believe you're terrific, others will believe it, too.

You've always got to remember, rock and roll's never been about giving up. For me, for a lot of kids, it was a totally positive force... not optimistic all the time, but positive. It was never—never—about surrender.

~*Bruce Springsteen*[17]

Don't ever let Imposter Syndrome take you out of the game. Bradley Voytek, a neuroscientist and featured TED speaker, uses the term to describe accomplished people who feel like they don't deserve their success.[18] When you start to notice all of the beautiful and brilliant folks around you, you start to think, "I'm not so special. I'll never be as good as all of these great people!" This happens often to individuals who have a few achievements under their belt and are working hard for more.

If you start to feel that way, it's time to crank it up. Put on your best spandex, grab your black leather jacket, and walk out there like a star. Remember, odds are that the people you envy are suffering from a little bit of Imposter Syndrome too. Swagger until you're cured.

A Chord Drill
"Mirror Check"

Keep a small mirror across from your desk at work. When you talk on the phone or to a visitor, take a quick, occasional look at your reflection. Make sure your posture is good, your expression is relaxed, and your eyes are up. A confident pose will carry into your voice, expressions, and conversation. Even if the other person can't see you, they will sense a difference. A quick look every now and again is perfect—no need to stare.

Playing Your A Chord

Practice your A chord every day. Find reasons to be confident and project that confidence to the people you encounter. Recognize fear when you feel it and resolve to push past feelings of inadequacy or intimidation when they tempt you to procrastinate or give up. Keep developing your skills so that you will be prepared when opportunities arise and be watching for them. Trust that if you do these things, you will be investing in and improving on yourself. Swagger a little. Your attitude will drive your actions, and these things will set you apart. That's the rock 'n' roll way of life that Lester Bangs was talking about.

Guitar Lesson 1
A Chord

Your A chord is a combination of:

- Your response to failure
- Your ability to seize opportunity
- Your swagger

Things to Remember

1. Failure is painful, but it is also an educational experience. Take what you learn and keep trying.
2. Nurture the persistence in your character.
3. You will miss some of the opportunities you reach for. You will miss <u>all</u> of the opportunities you <u>don't</u> reach for.
4. Develop your swagger. It is better to appear a little over confident than under-confident.
5. Practice your "instrument." Work on improving your knowledge, your information, and your brand every day.
6. Put your gold records on the wall. Make sure your successes are where people can see them. They will speak for themselves.

B Chord
BAND

As good as I am, I'm nothing without my band.

~ Steven Tyler[19]

Your A Chord is all about what's inside you. But your B Chord, your BAND, is all about making sweet music with other people. Musicians talk about those awesome moments where the sound is "tight," where all of the instruments and vocal elements blend together to create something greater than any one could create alone. That doesn't happen by accident; it's the result of hours of rehearsal, constant awareness, and collective consensus. If someone is having an off day, if two members are squabbling over the tempo, or if the drummer doesn't show up, the sound will suffer. It may still be good, especially if the individual members have great chops, but it won't be great. If you want to rock, your band matters as much as your attitude. You have to surround yourself with the right people, you have to create the right relationships with them, and you have to work together.

Who Is Your Band?

You may not live your life on a tour bus, but I'm willing to bet that somehow, some way you are involved in a band. What areas of your life demand collaboration to achieve results? The human resources director in a corporate office works with people across departments. Salespeople have a circle of managers and coworkers. A small business owner has to keep at least a couple of people on staff. A freelance writer has an agent, plus clients. An intramural softball coach has players all over the field. And what about your household? Do you have a spouse or significant other? Kids?

In all of these different situations, you must interact with others on a regular basis. Each person has different skills and a unique personality that impacts how you relate. You have to cooperate to get things done. You can ask for help to get things you want or need, and if you experience conflict, it can bring productivity to a grinding halt and make everyone miserable. Sounds like a band to me.

Some members, let's say the CEO or the parent, function like the drummer; they establish the rhythm that everyone follows and keep the beat. Others—support staff or assistant coaches for example—work like the bass player, adding strength to the beat and filling out the sound. Folks in middle management are like the rhythm guitar; they translate strategy into tactics and establish the pattern for the melody. Your lead guitar and your vocalists are the public face of enterprise—your sales force, your publicity folks, etc. The individuals and instruments may change from band to band, but one thing remains true: the music doesn't happen without everyone's participation.

B Chord Drill
"Map Your Band"

Think about the members of your team (or staff, or family), your band. What do they play? Not the specific instrument, per se. But what role do they fill in your operation?
Who sets the beat?
Who builds the sound?
Who establishes the melody?
Who sings out your message?
Write down your thoughts, and then ask your band what roles they think they play.

So we have established that your team, your co-workers, vendors, associates, employees, even your kids, can make up your band. Maybe your band members are limited to your department, maybe not. Maybe you chose them, or not. Maybe they're smarter than you are, or not. Whatever the specific make up of your band, you all have to be committed to the group's well-being in order to make music together. The most successful rock groups realize that they need to maintain the band—its operations, its image, its products— to stay on top. You can use the same strategies that a real rock band uses: create a vision, commit to the long haul, and take charge of change.

Chapter 4

VISION

Create a Vision

All the big bands began as little bands with a vision.

~Steven Tyler[20]

Aerosmith's front man, Steven Tyler, knows a little something about vision; his band grew from a local cover group into one of rock 'n' roll's longest-lived stadium acts. What took Aerosmith from a bunch of long-haired nobodies to legend status was having a strong, singular focus for their energy. They didn't just work hard, they worked *toward* something. A vision is a band's unifying force; it is a common purpose that everyone works toward. You use your vision to set goals, to motivate you, and to organize your efforts. If your vision is a clear one, humble beginnings, setbacks, and disappointments won't matter. It should be specific and well-articulated:

"We are going to become the trend-setters for the U.S. cell phone accessory market."

"We are going to re-define green building techniques."

"We are going to make the t-shirts that every kid under 18 will be wearing next season."

When KISS started their career in music, they agreed that they wanted to do more than stand in front of an audience and play. They wanted to create a complete spectacle. The costumes and makeup came out of that vision. In fact, they were so committed to perfecting the visual aspect of their performances that they went out and bought video equipment so they could record their rehearsals and perfect their stage moves. In the 1970s, that meant a huge financial investment in addition to the time and energy they put in. But the vision was so strong and clear that the whole band got behind it. And while they may not have any Grammys to their name, they are one of the top-grossing bands in rock 'n' roll history.[21]

Having vision is also what gets others talking about you. Live Nation CEO Michael Rapino describes rap star Jay-Z this way: "When we sat down with Jay-Z, 'How much money are you going to pay me?' came up in maybe the seventh conversation. The first conversation was, 'Can we change the business together?'" Jay-Z's vision (and the fact that he showed vision) was what inspired Live Nation to form a multi-million dollar partnership with him.[22]

Your vision doesn't have to be huge. It doesn't have to be in the distant future. It just has to be something your band can embrace. Once you have a vision, then you can focus on making plans and commitments.

Chapter 5

THE LONG TERM

Commit to the Long Haul

Even if your vision is, at the beginning, a modest one, your band has to have consensus and commitment. This is what gets you through the initial phase and on to the long-term pursuit of your ideas. Harvard psychologists have conducted research into teamwork that shows that the longer a group works together, the more effective they are. In fact, the more stable the line up of members, the more productive they will be over time. Such groups also benefit from strong leadership, someone who keeps their energies focused on the vision and gets them the resources and support they need.[23]

Individuals may or may not always get along. They may have very strong and differing opinions about how to get where you want to go. The band can weather those things as long as all members are willing to do what's best for the band when it's time. Some conflict and pushback can actually fuel your band's work. The same Harvard study shows more creative solutions generated in situations of managed conflict.

Consider the famously explosive relationship between Keith Richards and Mick Jagger. They have had well-documented shouting matches, have insulted one another repeatedly in the press and in public, and have gone through phases where they arrive separately for every gig on a tour. And yet the band has been going for about 50 years. (Seriously—since 1962!) These two men, both known for having strong opinions and even stronger wills, put their personal issues aside when they get on stage. Keith Richards has summed it up, "This thing is bigger than both of us."[24] Your vision should inspire that kind of commitment, the kind that can make people push through pain, anger, disappointment, and failure, because they want to be there when that vision becomes reality.

If everyone is committed to doing what's best for the band, and has the vision clearly fixed in their minds, you will be in a much better position to deal with any difficulties that come your way. When you do come up against an obstacle, take the time to analyze it and learn to appreciate the difference between a momentary setback and a genuine problem. You will find that lots of things that feel like a big problem in the moment often turn out to be temporary setbacks. Here's an acid test:

- Can money fix it?
- In time, will it go away?
- Is it the product of one person's actions?

2011

If the answer to any of these questions is "yes", chances are you are dealing with a momentary setback. You can then take action to make a quick recovery: find sources of funding, wait it out, offer the person a chance to make it right or walk away, etc.

If you are dealing with a genuine problem, it's time to call a band meeting and strategize.

Problem or setback, when obstacles come your way you should also take time to consider the possibilities. We all have to deal with things that we'd rather not face—offers that aren't as good as we want, plans that don't turn out as well as we hoped. Failures tend to glow like neon; they're highly visible and seem to dominate the landscape. But the negative aspects of a situation can block your vision. Problems aren't typically bigger than opportunities; they're just easier to spot. The positive aspects of a dilemma or difficulty take a bit more insight...a little more digging...a little more time. But chances are, they <u>are</u> there. As your band develops the ability to draw these out, they will give you the material you need to enact your own change.

Chapter 6

TAKE CHARGE OF CHANGE

Enact Your Own Change

Everybody has accepted by now that change is unavoidable. But that still implies that change is like death and taxes: it should be postponed as long as possible and no change would be vastly preferable. But in a period of upheavals, such as the one we are living in, change is the norm.

~Peter Drucker[25]

The late management expert Peter Drucker really got it right, didn't he? We believe that change is inevitable in our professional and personal lives, and that it is usually a bad thing. We will be dealing with change as its own chord at a later point. For now, what matters is making sure that your band has the right attitude about it. That means being able to respond successfully when situations or circumstances change. But more importantly, it means being capable of enacting change in a creative, proactive way. Remember, songs don't write or play themselves. BANDS make them happen.

No matter who you are, no matter what you did, no matter where you've come from, you can always change, become a better version of yourself.

~ Madonna[26]

Let's look at two of the most successful and high-paid women in the music industry: Madonna and Lady Gaga. Both pop divas are known for their rapidly-evolving style and over the top personas, and for successfully penetrating markets well beyond music: book publishing, fashion clothing, endorsements, even advocacy for social causes. A unifying factor in their success is that both performers see themselves and their art as work-in-progress. They actively experiment with new ideas and techniques. They try on different guises and move bravely into new media. Instead of simply responding to social shifts, they actively change themselves. This strategy helps these women stand at the cutting edge of society. For Madonna, it has given her the ability to stay relevant and popular for more than 20 years. For Lady Gaga, it gave her an entrance into the market. She was able to test different modes until she found one that clicked with the public. She then went from being a virtual unknown to #1 on the Forbes list of top grossing acts in under 5 years.[27]

I've been popular and unpopular, successful and unsuccessful, loved and loathed, and I know how meaningless it all is. Therefore, I feel free to take whatever risks I want.

~ Madonna[28]

I would not be able to breathe if I couldn't make art. I just wouldn't. Look at me. This is me on a normal day. I wake up in the morning, and I make my hairbow, and I put my cat suit on, and I call up everybody in the Haus of Gaga, and I say, "How are we gonna be brilliant today?"

~ Lady Gaga[29]

It's a fantastic question. What could happen if you asked yourself that same question every day? What might your band say if you ask them?

Challenging yourselves is one of the healthiest things you can do as a band. In fact, current research on creativity and entrepreneurship suggests that sticking too closely to established ways of doing things can block creativity and make people less able to cope with change.[30] Basically, when the standard method of handling things doesn't work for the current problem, they freeze up. Hey, if you play nothing but the same songs over and over, eventually your ability to write new music will deteriorate. To keep yourselves fresh, you must continually challenge yourselves not to do things the same old way. Don't wait for your methods to stop working before you feel motivated to try.

B Chord Drill
Brainstorm Brilliant

Every day, ask yourself "How am I going to be brilliant today? Tomorrow? Every day from now on?" Spend five minutes jotting down ideas. Encourage your band to do the same. Once a week (or month, if time is expensive), get together for a coffee or a beer and share what you have written down.

Like Madonna and Gaga, your band should not only be unafraid of change, but excited about the possibility of making change. If you are functioning well as a group, and everyone is on the same page about your vision and your commitment to pursuing it in the long-term, then the odds are good that the excitement will happen naturally. You'll sound tight when you play your current hits, and you will be ready to write the new music, too.

B Chord Drill
Your Band's Greatest Hits

This is an exercise you should do in a group. Get the members of your band together (your staff, your department or team, your family). Spend a few moments talking about the things you do well as a group. Then ask them what they consider your "greatest hits" to be. What have your greatest successes been? Your most memorable moments? What are the things the people are going to remember you for (the songs that will be played on classic rock stations for years to come)?

Next, ask them about what they think your "new songs" should be. What would they like to try doing as a team? Are there new technologies, methods, or markets? Are there new "instruments" they would like to learn to play or a new medium to explore? What skills does your band have to bring to a new song? What will you have to learn?

Bands, like other successful organizations, function best if they master the balance between stability and flexibility. The ideal mix is:

- A stable line up (a core of competent members who stick with you through the years);
- A single and compelling idea that drives the whole group's efforts;
- And a collective ability to produce appealing and high quality work in new situations as well as familiar territory.

A band can keep rockin' for 30 years as long as it maintains its vision, stays focused on the long-term, and creates its own change. Your band will still face challenges, go through rough patches, and experience some strife. But in the end you will be much more satisfied and fulfilled individually and as a group. You will be a lot happier. And, you will be better positioned to keep your fans happy. Rock stars live and die by their fans, you know. That's the subject of our next chord.

Guitar Lesson 2
B Chord

Your band is composed of the people with whom you are working on a common project or goal. You can be in several bands at once: your family, your office, and your volunteer organization, for example.

Band success depends on:

- Creating a vision
- Committing to the long term
- Enacting change

Things to Remember:

1. A good vision focuses your energy and sense of purpose. It doesn't have to be a big vision to start, just a clear one.
2. When conflict or differences of opinion come up, commit to doing what's best for the band.
3. Remember that songs don't write or play themselves. Bands make them happen.
4. Focus on both your greatest hits and on creating new material.

F Chord
FANS

Vitamin F (The Secret to Rock Star Nutrition)

In rock 'n' roll, you don't have to have a top 10 hit to be a success. You can have a long and happy career without ever getting nominated for a single award. It's also possible to become a millionaire without ever signing with a label. Hey, you can even be an international celebrity while the critics denounce you as a talentless hack. You can become a rock star without any of the standard accomplishments, as long as you have one essential element: You have to get your vitamin F everyday if you want to grow up and be a big star. And that brings us to our F chord: FANS. No fans, no stardom. It's that simple. They pay your salary when they buy what you sell, and they keep you and your business going by spreading the word.

How Fans Sustain Bands (and Brands)

Rock 'n' roll stardom, much like any other business, is built on brand loyalty. Why does the One Hit Wonder fade into obscurity? Because people like the initial product/song, but do not care enough for the brand to come back for more. Whatever interest might have driven the momentary success, subsequent songs do not create a strong connection between listeners and the band. Consequently, airplay decreases, album sales dwindle, and concert attendance drops. If musicians cannot build brand loyalty and repeat business, it does not matter how talented or dedicated they are. Eventually, their band will fizzle out. A solid fan base makes all the difference.

To build a fan base, it isn't enough that people like you and what you do. People don't drive across three states in a station wagon with eight friends for something that they just like. A fan is someone <u>devoted</u>; someone who not only enjoys your work, but cares deeply about it. It has value; it adds meaning and pleasure to her life. A fan's enthusiasm goes well beyond occasionally buying your product off the shelf or mentioning you at a party. A fan understands what your work is about (maybe even better than you), knows your band inside and out, and loves telling other people about you. He wants to share his enthusiasm, encourage other people to check you out, and help promote your success. Why? Because the more opportunities you get, the more of your product will be out there for him to enjoy. If you are truly good at fan relations, promoting you makes him feel a part of something, and he will celebrate your growth as if it were his own.

It's true for music, it's true for business, and it's true for your homeowner's association. The people who believe passionately in Brand You are the people who are going to refer you. They invest their money in your products or services. They stay informed about your activities. They help you get elected and win awards. They are the people who post pictures of you on their social media sites, tweet and post updates on what you're doing, carry copies of your business card in their bags, and generally get your message out to the world. Not only do you need them to survive, it is through them that you thrive.

Listen to the words of another star, one of Hollywood's most durable and versatile leading men:

The people out there who watch the films. They're the only reason I'm here. They're the ones who keep me employed. They're my employer. It's not Disney; it's not anybody else.

~Johnny Depp[31]

Depp's not dissing Disney, of course. But, he is acknowledging that long-term success comes from continued demand. As long as people want to see him in movies, he has a job. So it behooves him to be mindful of them and to remember their part in his career.

It's All About Connections

When a person likes you and your product, you have a window of opportunity for creating a connection. You get their attention with a "hit single," whatever that is for your particular situation: a good product, a stellar presentation, a well-written editorial, or a killer software program. From there, you and your band should be focused on three things: conversion, cultivation and mobilization.

Chapter 7

Find Your Fans

No, I always felt that amongst my core fans....they fundamentally understood the values that are at work in my work.

~Bruce Springsteen[32]

Let's talk about the conversion process first. How do you convert listeners to fans? First you have to understand who your fans are. Whether you and your band have just gotten together, or find yourselves at a crossroads with a need to reassess, it is imperative that you should learn about your fans. If you don't know who they are, how can you find them? How will you reach them?

You have already started working on this—though you may not know it—because it starts with knowing yourself and your band. So far, I have asked you to reflect on yourself and your team. You know what your skills and gifts are, you are all on the same page about your product offering, and you have a clear vision for what you want to accomplish with those things. Now it is time to ask a key question: "Who wants what we have to offer?"

Demographics Are Just the Beginning

If you have any business savvy, if you didn't sleep through your marketing classes in college, then you already know the importance of researching your demographic. What does your typical consumer look like? How old are they? What do they like to wear? Where do they shop? Which TV shows are their favorites? You can bet that the record executives at the major labels ask these questions when they are deciding how to promote an artist or whether to produce a record.

Smart bands do this too, especially as they are starting out. Even a completely naïve musician understands that if you play emo rock and the gig turns out to be at a country bar, you could be in for a long and uncomfortable night. Where possible, bands try to book themselves into venues that are popular with the audience they want to reach. They make t-shirts with designs that they think those people will like. They put up posters in the restaurants and stores where those people shop. There is actually a cottage industry of consultants and training programs to help musicians perform demographic research and position their music as a marketable product.

But demographic data will only get you so far. Don't get me wrong! Market research is an important tool and you neglect it at your peril. But you can't look at a demographic profile as the sum of what you need to know. A demographic is not a person; it is a statistical summary. Numbers aren't fans, people are. It may help your band decide where your target market hangs out, but once you book the gig, it is up to you to get them to listen. You've got to play songs they want to hear! And if you do get their attention, you've got to draw them in and hold them; make them want more. You have to instill them with the belief that if they stick with you, there will be more of those songs to come.

Ultimately, you are seeking to trigger a conversion. You want each person who comes into contact with your work to go from being a bystander to being a listener (or a buyer, if you like) to being a fan.

BYSTANDER ----> LISTENER ----> FAN

There's actually a body of research on how this happens. Here's a quick and helpful summary:

The management research team of Bloemer and Kasper speaks of a process among consumers. It begins with a single purchase, where someone chooses your product or service for the first time. If they come back for more, that's called "repeat purchase behavior." But there comes a point where "consumers bind themselves to products or services as a result of a deep-seated commitment." Basically, the decision to buy from you takes on a very personal dimension.[33]

Jack Trout is an eminent expert on branding and psychology. When he applied statistical data on brain to purchasing activity, he discovered that humans can't actually process the continual stream of information that our environments throw at us. In order to make decision-making easier on a daily basis, we create a store of information about what we want and why. When certain things fit those criteria, we are more likely to notice them and to respond.[34]

So actually, human beings are *wired* to become fans. We crave the stability and satisfaction of having consistent access to things we want from someone we trust. So if someone hears you playing their song, they'll tune in. If you can come to understand what they want and provide it for them on a regular basis, they will love you for it. If you can introduce them to new and entertaining/useful stuff along the way, they'll come to rely on you and encourage others to do the same. The flip side of that equation is that people tend to tune out anything that doesn't feel relevant to their lives. Somehow, you have to get through the static, get their attention, and win their loyalty.

I want anyone who spends money on us to be really pleased with their purchase.

~ Chris Martin[35]

Coldplay's Chris Martin may phrase things in a way that would bother some of his contemporaries—there are still a lot of artists out there who balk at the idea of considering their music a product or purchase—but his attitude is one that every business should emulate. You <u>should</u> want your buyers to be happy with their experience. Bring the rock star mentality with you into all aspects of your life, and the same should be true with everyone you encounter. Your charity commitments should be happy with your volunteer service. Your friends should be happy with your interpersonal encounters. Your kids should be happy with their experience of you as a parent (within reason, of course). Wanting good things for other people and working to make their lives better is a basic human responsibility. So if you want to rock your career and your life that should be a default assumption. Start by striving for everyone to be "pleased with their purchase." Then reach for something more.

Basically, our MO was that after every gig, whether we were a support band or if we were headlining a 2000 seat venue, or playing in a strange little venue... after a show, no matter what, we would always sign [autographs].

~ Amanda Palmer[36]

Not everybody knows Amanda Palmer, but her fans certainly do. She may not be a household name, but she's an indie darling with 20,000 Facebook fans and 40,000 Twitter followers. Palmer is a true poster child for successful fan cultivation. It started with her work with the Dresden Dolls, the band she references in the quotation above, and their belief that direct contact with concert-goers was the key to building lasting relationships. If the audience liked your performance, then autograph signing after the show was a great way to solidify those relationships. She and her collaborators committed to doing so no matter the size or success of the individual show.

Direct contact is vital to growing an initial fan base. To convert people from bystanders to fans, there are several steps you must take.

1. *Do your background research.* Start with the market and demographic data.
2. *Hang out where they are.* Spend time in the places frequented by the folks you want to reach.
3. *Talk to them.* Ask them what they care about. Ask them what they like, and why they like it. Pay attention.
4. *Show them your stuff.* It can be a product, a service, even an idea. Find a few articulate "fan prototypes" and let them see what you're working on.
5. *Ask for their feedback.* Ask what they like about it. Ask what they would change or improve. Ask how much they would be willing to pay for something similar. (Note: Don't ask for a yes/no response to "would you buy this?" The answer might not be truthful, especially if they like you.)

Winning fans is important. You need to direct meaningful attention to the task of converting bystanders to fans, and to maintain that priority even as your band starts to rise in the charts.

You should reach out continually to connect with new audiences. But remember, even as you seek to reach new fans, your existing fans also deserve your respect and attention. Once those connections are made, they will require nurturing. Rock stars are able to keep fans over the long-term and remember, that's an important goal for your band.

F Chord Drill
Interview Your Ideal Fan

Find a couple of folks among your friends and acquaintances who represent your ideal fans. Ask them to participate in a mock interview with you. These people will portray the part of the "fan" and you will be the "rock star." Let them know that the situation is fictional, but that the responses should be genuine and honest. With your idea, product, or service in mind, prepare a series of questions. Do any market research you might need in advance! Sit down with your ideal fans and interview them about what attracts them, what holds their interest, and what inspires their loyalty. Share the results with your band. If you want to expand the field, ask band members to complete a similar interview with the ideal fan of their choice.

Chapter 8

Keep Your Fans

Real musicians and real fans stay together for a long, long time.

~Bonnie Raitt[37]

We're the McDonald's of rock. We're always there to satisfy, and a billion served.

~Paul Stanley, KISS[38]

If all it took to be a rock star was getting someone to love you for a week, then there would be no One Hit Wonders. But if you and your band are going to commit to a long-term strategy, then you need to prepare for a relationship that lasts. If you want to keep your fans, you need to cultivate your fans. So first, you need to view your connection to fans <u>as</u> a relationship. Does this mean that you let them crash on your couch for weeks on end, or borrow your car? No, that probably means that someone's got some boundary issues.

But you do need to embrace a certain social agreement between you and your fans:

- First, there is give and take. They offer you their attention, their financial support, and their presence. You offer them a quality product or experience.
- Second, there is sharing. You exchange information. You tell them when and where they can find you, what you are doing, and cool stuff they should know. They tell you how to contact them, what they want to know, and what they care about.
- Third, there is mutual respect and affection. Fans already have an emotional connection to you. They admire your gifts and acknowledge the value you bring to their lives. In return, you should be warm and polite in your interactions. Listen to their ideas. Respond when they communicate. (If you ever feel uncomfortable because a fan is stepping over the line personally or professionally, address it directly but nicely. Respond in a firm, polite, and legally appropriate way.)

Like Johnny Depp, you need to keep in mind that you have a certain position because there are people who are invested in keeping you there. You depend on them for the realization of your vision, for your livelihood, and for your ongoing ability to create your work.

Keeping your fans means keeping them satisfied. Fortunately for you, this is not a moving target, unlike most of our love lives. There are some guidelines you can follow.

1. Be Thankful

It just gets draining on a person being in the papers every day. So I was like, I'm gonna come back here. I want to talk to all the people, the fans. I want to let them know how much I appreciate all their support.

~ *Sean "Puff Daddy" Combs*[39]

Your fans want to know that you value their investment of time, attention, and money. After all, they value what you offer them. So say thank you. Find small ways to give back—one-on-one meetings, notes, coupons, merchandise freebies, a sponsored coffee break. The method is up to you, but make the effort.

2. Be Accessible

Fans are my favorite thing in the world. I've never been the type of artist who has that line drawn between their friends and their fans. The line's always been really blurred for me. I'll hang out with them after the show. I'll hang out with them before the show. If I see them in the mall, I'll stand there and talk to them for 10 minutes.

~*Taylor Swift*[40]

There is a basic etiquette that exists between rock stars and their fans. A star never refuses a reasonable request for an autograph or photo opportunity. In return, fans don't bug them at inopportune moments say, when they're eating at a restaurant, or walking into a public bathroom. In your situation, you may never have to flee from an overexcited group of Japanese schoolgirls, but you should make time to interact with the people who are invested in your work. If you see them in public places, take the time to chat. Be sure to engage: make eye contact, ask questions, and show with your body language that you are paying attention and you care. Open various channels of communication with them: letters, e-mail, blog, Facebook, Twitter. If they contact you, offer an individualized response from a real human being. Nothing will turn your fans off quicker than an auto-reply, except maybe no reply at all.

3. Be a Mutual Admiration Society:

Coldplay fans are the best in the world. If you like Coldplay then you're obviously very intelligent and good looking and all-around brilliant.

~Chris Martin[41]

Yes, Chris Martin's comment is a bit tongue-in-cheek, but it is smart, too. Showing confidence in your fans also demonstrates confidence in your band and your brand. Compliment them on their dedication and on their engagement with the world and your field. If someone tells you of a success they have achieved with your help, publicize it and congratulate them. Use your communication channels to praise them for their own accomplishments and for their efforts to support you. (Make sure you have their permission to do this first.)

4. Be Responsive:

As for questions and feedback, you can do this during face-to-face meetings, via surveys, or through various communication channels. Ask your fans what they think, what they need, and what they want. Listen closely and implement good ideas. If they point you in the direction of a new development, technology, idea, or market, then follow up and educate yourself about it. Be open to learning from them.

And if they are unhappy about something, take the time to comfort and validate them. Listen and investigate complaints. Offer apologies when necessary and explanations where appropriate.

Lady Gaga regularly responds to her fans on her Twitter feed. If she hears criticism of a performance, or an expression of disappointment, she sends a tweet quickly to affirm her commitment to providing what they expect.

5. Be Proactive

If your fans are buzzing about something, explore it. If you discover something new and exciting, share it with them. Open an information exchange. Build enthusiasm by giving them advance notice of upcoming products or activities. Ask them for their help in spreading the word.

If you see an opportunity to meet demand, fill it! When it came to the attention of KISS band members that their fans had started holding conventions, they offered to step in and sponsor an official convention of their own. Instead of threatening to shut down unlicensed activity, they offered an enhanced experience based on the things their fans had created themselves. It opened the door to a whole new marketing channel for the band.

When you engage in these activities, pledge yourselves to doing them well. If you do something for your fans, go all in; don't stop short or make half-hearted gestures. Don't start projects that you can't complete, and don't throw yourself into something without forethought. True fans will forgive you the occasional flub, but if you consistently give them the impression of ambivalence by making your contact with them lukewarm or half-hearted, they will begin to feel that their affection for you is unrequited. There's only so much love a fan will give you if you don't return it.

For all that, you should embrace your fans instead of fearing them. Remember, they are predisposed to love you—that's what being a fan means. If you keep the quality of your work high, stay consistent about your vision, and invest yourself in cultivating a warm relationship with them, they will do just about anything you ask. In them, you will have a tremendous source of energy and effort that you can mobilize to promote yourself.

Chapter 9

Mobilize Your Fans

Okay, so we've talked about how to convert and cultivate your fans. Both of those activities are important, but they really only set the stage for our third key activity, mobilization. I'd define mobilization as the art of turning your fans' enthusiasm for you into action.

At this point, you might be asking yourself "Why does it matter who supports me or for how long?" As long as *someone* keeps buying your products and services, votes for you, or renews your contract, does it really matter who it is? Absolutely! Because your fans have much greater potential than just monetization. If you treat them well and you empower them, they will become your best marketers and advocates. They create scalability that you and your band can only dream about on your own.

Remember the Dead

Think back to the story about the Grateful Dead in Chapter 2—empowering their fans to bring recording equipment to their shows. Not only did they generate good will by demonstrating openness in a particularly tense and mercenary situation, they increased their own visibility through fans who wanted to share their experiences.

If you've managed relations well, your fans should be ready and waiting for opportunities to help you. They should be independently sharing your work with others—find ways to invite them to do this. Offer links to freebies on your website, host networking events and let them bring friends. Keep in mind that you want them to view this as an opportunity to participate with you in something. It shouldn't feel like the biannual beg-a-thon from public radio.

I'd like to hone in on a single case study on the possibilities of mobilizing your fan base, an artist who embodies multiple options for involving them in your vision and goals: Amanda Palmer.[42]

The Case of Amanda Palmer

I mentioned Palmer briefly in Chapter 7 in reference to the Dresden Dolls and their commitment to post-show autographs. Palmer has managed to create a vibrant boutique niche for herself in the music scene. She may not top the charts, and photographers don't always recognize her on the red carpet. But she has thousands of exceedingly loyal and personally invested fans. She communicates with them through a variety of social media in addition to her music and deploys them across a range of situations.

Drawing a Crowd

Palmer frequently uses Twitter and her blog to publicize events, especially on a tight deadline. If she finds herself with a free night, wants to generate excitement for an underpublicized gig, or just feels bored, she sends out a mass message. She informs her fans where she will be, what the nature of the event is, and occasionally invites them to participate in some direct way (costumes, props, showing up to a random spot). By tweeting an invitation to one secret gig one morning, she gathered an audience of 350 people that same night for a piano concert at a warehouse.

Generating Excitement and Income

While home on a Friday night, Palmer sent out a message about being bored and lonely. A group of her fans responded, and they began a playful conversation that soon expanded to an Internet event. As a joke, she quickly sketched out a t-shirt design for the fictional movement started in the conversation. When fan interest spiked, she sent the design to a friend with a printing business. He created a simple website to sell the product, and launched it in less than an hour. In the next 48 hours, they collected $11,000 in profits from the orders. Fans got a souvenir from the event; Palmer got some cash and publicity for her personal brand.

Go to the Mattresses

Nobody wants to get in a public conflict or legal battle, and if you do, it is best to aim for a compromise solution that doesn't involve your fans. However, their support and efforts can be a powerful tool for shaping a public narrative.

In 2008, Palmer released a video in which she wore a midriff-baring costume. Executives at her record label pointed out her untoned abs, and wanted to remove any shots with her exposed belly. They explained that they found the costume unflattering and thought her soft stomach detracted from the sex appeal of the video. Palmer resisted the cuts, insisting that this sent the wrong message about body image and musical priorities. After she notified her network about the situation and her feelings, fans responded with collective action that solidified into the "ReBELLYon." They built a website that publicized the controversy, took photographs of their own bellies and sent them to record executives, and eventually published "The Belly Book", which featured photos and personal stories from over 600 fans.

Not a bad track record for a Boston girl who has yet to score a gold record!

Your relationship with your fans should be unique; it should be true to the standards and the vision of your band. In the words of the Boss, your fans should understand your core values. It would obviously not be appropriate for every organization to expect or request the kind of advocacy that Palmer's fans displayed. You should encourage your fans to speak and act on your behalf because that's what mobilizing them means. But it is also important to show sensitivity for their comfort level and keep their energies focused in positive directions.

F Chord Drill
Post Card Love

Contact your fans and invite them to send you a post card from a favorite site. It can be a card from their business, town, a beloved vacation spot, etc. Ask them to share something that your work has meant to them or offered them. Display the post cards in your office, and scan digital images of them to post to a website or social media site. Offer a small prize for the best image and best story.

Playing Your F Chord

Loyal fans are the secret to health, influence and longevity. The other basic chords can become a little automatic, at least for certain periods of time, and you'll be able to play them without thinking. But the F chord requires diligent practice and mindful effort. Learn about the people that you want to become your fans and play their songs. When you've successfully converted them, dedicate yourself to keeping those relationships strong and warm. If you nurture them, your fans will nurture you. Embrace the fact that they are waiting (even longing) for an opportunity to help you. Ask for their input and participation. Be a responsible rock star, and take their best interests to heart even as you send them out to spread the word. It should be a beautiful, rewarding relationship for everyone involved!

Guitar Lesson 3
F Chord

To be a rock star, you need loyal fans. Period.

To maintain a successful fan base, you must master three things:

- Conversion
- Cultivation
- Mobilization.

Things to Remember:

1. The basic equation for stardom is:

   BYSTANDER ----> LISTENER ----> FAN

2. You need to develop in depth knowledge of your fans. Get to know your fans as a demographic, and then as people.
3. Start by wanting people to be pleased with their interactions with you and your work, then reach for something more.

4. Maintain an active, engaged relationship with your fans.

5. Keep a two-way channel of communication open. Share your news and information with them, and let them share with you.

6. Whatever you do for your fans, do it with enthusiasm. Do it well.

7. Empower your fans to help you.

Section 2 – The Chords That Add Color & Depth

G Chord
GOALS

Into the great wide open
Under the skies of blue
Out in the great wide open
A rebel without a clue
~ Tom Petty, "Into the Great Wide Open"[43]

In Tom Petty's song "Into the Great Wide Open," a young rock 'n' roller named Eddie gets a chance at stardom. He has some talent, a bit of luck, and releases a hit record. But Tom reminds us throughout the song that Eddie is ultimately "a rebel without a clue," and at the end of the song, his future is uncertain. If you watch the video, the end is even sadder as you watch his life implode. Eddie doesn't seem to have much control over his own life; he just drifts along, and the end result is that he wastes his talent and opportunities. Know anybody who has done that? We all do; that's why the song speaks to us.

You and your band want to avoid that path. You need to have a vision that guides you, or else you will all end up "rebels without a clue." If you're playing your B chord well, you have already got that part locked down. You have a clearly articulated dream and everyone is on board with pursuing it. That means it's time to start practicing your G chord, and setting yourselves some <u>GOALS</u>.

Goals enable you to put your vision into action. They take a big idea and transform it into a series of practical steps. Make and keep specific goals, and you will be well on your way to achieving and keeping rock star status. Fumble your goals, or forget them, and you may not even get the chance to be a One Hit Wonder. That's not what you want; what you want is a wall full of gold records that you can admire every day. With the help of some of rock 'n' roll's most successful stars, we can determine a strategy for creating objectives that you can reach, executing steps as a team, responding to obstacles, and encouraging adaptability.

Chapter 10

GO FOR THE GOALS

Of course I'm ambitious. What's wrong with that? Otherwise you sleep all day.

~Ringo Starr[44]

The self-confidence one builds from achieving difficult things and accomplishing goals is the most beautiful thing of all.

~ Madonna[45]

Madonna may be the best model for rock star goal setting alive. You can be a nobody from Michigan who moves to New York and makes a momentary splash. That has happened often enough in the entertainment industry. But to be idolized, criticized, and emulated all over the world, you have to set your sights a bit higher. Her career in music has lasted several decades; she has international respect as a smart businesswoman in addition to being a savvy artist. To do that, you need to set big, bold, audacious goals.

Rock your BHAG

Are you familiar with the term BHAG? It has been floating around corporate and motivational circles for years now. It stands for "big hairy audacious goal." The concept dares people and organizations to dream big, to set your sights on the very best possible outcome for yourself and your organization. Your vision can be a manifestation of this. Your swagger is what will give you the guts to live in hope and expectation of achieving it. The Grateful Dead's BHAG was to be considered the only band in their niche. KISS's BHAG is to rock their fans with a full spectrum experience that no other band can match. Can you and your band articulate something that expresses your idea of the wildest success imaginable

Dream On, Dream On, Dream On
Dream until your dreams come true.
~Aerosmith[46]

G Chord Drill
Dream On

Sit down with your band and ask the question "what is your idea of the hugest success imaginable?" What would it look like for you to succeed beyond your wildest dreams? Really imagine and describe it. Get specific. Get silly if you need to. But get it out there. Write it out. Keep it close and read it every now and again.

I said in Chapter 4 that your vision does not have to be grand, and that's true. If you and your band want to start out with something less scary than a full-on BHAG, that's fine. You have to find a jumping off point that works for all of you at this moment. But keep this in mind on the journey: there is little satisfaction in achieving a goal that you know is within easy reach. If you get there, there's no surprise or deep satisfaction. But if you fail, you will probably beat yourself up. If you fail at a huge goal, there's still a certain satisfaction in having tried. You don't tend to kick yourself over it. And if you do succeed? Well, then you really have a reason to be proud.

We're trying to do something new; we're trying to be the greatest group in the world, and that also means the biggest. At the same time, we're trying to be radical-I mean, we never want to be really respectable—and maybe the two can't coexist, but we'll try.

~ *Joe Strummer, the Clash*[47]

The Plan of Action

If you're climbing the ladder of life, you go rung by rung, one step at a time. Don't look too far up, set your goals high but take one step at a time. Sometimes you don't think you're progressing until you step back and see how high you've really gone.

~Donny Osmond[48]

Wait a minute, did I just quote Donny Osmond? That cheesy guy from the '70s? Before you go dissing the Donny, let me tell you that the guy had 5 top ten hits before his 21st birthday, staged a successful comeback in the early 1990s, moved into a successful career on Broadway, and won on *Dancing with the Stars* in 2009. Now that's a rock star who knows how to stay focused, long after your critics tell you that your days are done.

Let's talk about that idea of climbing the ladder one step at a time. What does that mean for a rock band? It means completing a set of ongoing tasks to perfect your sound, get the word out, and get fans.

Create a Set List

Every band has a collection of songs they play. That's true whether they write their own stuff, use material someone wrote for them, or stick to covers. Those songs may be in various stages of development; before the band records or heads to a gig, they need to decide which are ready for public consumption and which need more work. The ones that are deemed ready, or at least ready for a test drive and feedback, are placed on a set list. There is often a serious discussion of the order in which to play songs, so that stronger material is interspersed with "iffier" stuff in a way that seems likely to get and hold the audience's attention. This list is the reference point for the band's performing activities. The set list is under constant revision as the band learns from their experiences. If one song bombs, it gets moved or removed. If another song does surprisingly well, the band puts it in an advantageous slot.

These conversations work best when they are open, honest, analytical, and cordial. If someone is having trouble learning a chord change, he should speak up. If the vocal is flat on that tune, the singer should be told. If the bass player noticed audience members dozing off during songs 3 and 4, everyone ought to talk about what that means. People can be very vulnerable during these conversations, so a healthy band has to balance frankness with appropriate vocabulary and tone.

You should do the same with your own products, services, or ideas. Which ones are your strongest? Which need more development? Which ones should be removed from your repertoire? You and your band should have intentional, serious discussions about these things. If you are running for public office, you have to talk about your message and ideas. If you are selling hard drives for small electronics, you have to discuss everything from the products themselves to how you are marketing them. If you don't take the time to get on the same page, you won't know what you are going to play when you get on stage. (Incidentally, that's when embarrassing public arguments tend to occur.) Share information, point out problems, and discuss solutions and new ideas. This should be done on a regular basis and is especially important after any "gig," that is, any significant event or activity that you undertake.

Get very good at what you do and some day you may be able to try what Elvis Costello did for his "The Wheel" tour. A giant spin wheel dominated the stage and the band would play whatever song turned up at the end of a spin. Imagine what it would be like if you knew all of your songs that well and had that much confidence in the quality of each one? How awesome would that be?

Rehearse

I have a friend who once worked with the Eagles. Glenn Frey told him that they never played a song at a live concert until they had played it perfectly 100 times in a row during rehearsals. Hard to believe? Well, it is certainly hard to emulate, but it demonstrates a rock star level of dedication and preparation. Anybody might get a lucky break, but you don't get to be the best by accident. A tight sound comes out of consistent, disciplined rehearsal. Each member is accountable for staying limber on his own instrument, and for following through on the responsibilities he is given.

Then, when you come together as a team, everyone will be prepared for the work that needs to be done.

Imagine what it would be like if you all practiced your best PowerPoint presentation 100 times in a row. Your sales calls? What if you practiced the protocols for your software beta test? What about your responses to questions in a debate? You would be more confident, better prepared, and more poised. Consider the benefits of rehearsing a facility tour of your building while preparing for an important visitor. Imagine how much smoother Christmas morning might go if you and your kids practiced what to say to Grandma when they opened their presents!

There are two basic lessons here:

- First, we tend to get better at tasks with embodied repetition (that means acting things out) and familiarity. You and your band should commit yourselves to doing whatever it takes to be the best at what you do. Want the tight sound? Become a well-oiled machine.

When I was younger, studying classical music, I really had to put in the time. Three hours a day is not even nice - you have to put in six.

~ *Alicia Keys*[49]

- Second, when success comes your way, you cannot afford to let the discipline slide. (Think of poor Whitney Houston!) Tickets for Eagles concerts are some of the most expensive on the market. Do you want your fans to think that you're dialing it in? Or worse, that you've lost it? Maybe Glenn Frey was onto something after all...

Schedule Gigs, Release Songs

A musician may be a master lyricist. She may have a golden voice and blistering guitar licks. She may be the best female artist since Joan Jett. But if no one ever hears her play, *no one will ever know*. In order to become a rock star, she has to get her music out there. If she's painfully shy and doesn't want to leave the house, she might find an eventual career as a songwriter and let others record her music. But she won't be a rock star. She has got to schedule gigs and get out there where people can see her play. At the very least, she's got to get her music on the Internet and radio where people can hear it. The music must enter the public sphere.

You are no different. Your might have a cutting edge idea. You might be a genius with numbers. You could be the best dad in the world. Your small business may have the sexiest product known to man, but if you don't put the word out, no one will ever know. So you need to schedule some gigs, and release some singles. Start sharing your ideas and information with others. Make opportunities to participate in a public forum. Remember, when you do that you need to go where your fans are and play their song.

G Chord Drill
The worst That Could Happen

Are you getting ready to launch a project or idea? Get a few friends together and tell them your fears about the worst thing that could happen. Then ask them to meet with you in 24 hours so you can make a presentation as though they were your actual target market. Suggest that they brainstorm ways of being the "nightmare" audience.

When you meet up again, make your presentation and have them act out that role; invite them to do their worst. It will give you an opportunity to strategize under adversity and develop poise under pressure. Since these are your friends, you can trust that you won't end up in the emergency room.

Make Conscious Connections

Play your G and your F interchangeably; you need them both to make sweet music. As you build your set list, rehearse, and play your gigs, do so with the conscious intention of building and maintaining your fan base. Make the commitment to keep people informed of your doings at every step. Create opportunities for your supporters and potential clients to interact with you. Plan small and intentional acts of gratitude; respond when they make contact, and follow up on any leads they give you. Carry your cards or publicity materials everywhere you go. (Musicians always have a few bumper stickers in their cases and backpacks. Always.) Be available to people; answer e-mails and messages. If you really want to make an impression, send the occasional handwritten thank you note.

Whatever strategy your band creates to maintain communication with your fans, make sure it is a conscious strategy. Be consistent about it. Listen to your fans and make alterations as necessary. Never let it fall by the wayside.

Hold a Release Party

This is important for both your band and your fans. When a project comes to fruition, make sure to announce it with a bit of fanfare, and turn that fanfare into a celebration. It takes hard work to turn an idea into an action, and your band deserves a chance to show off. Plus, people like an excuse for a party. It's an easy way to get your fans to turn out and build excitement.

In the age of social media, this does not always have to be a brick-and-mortar shindig, you know. If you give them a fun and creative premise, people can have a ball posting to a Facebook wall or Twitter feed. So, consider making some of your "release party" events a web-based project. They are inexpensive to execute, and people will be inclined to share when it is easy and they have a small contribution of their own to show off.

Be Ready to Change Course

Map out your future, but do it in pencil.

~Jon Bon Jovi[50]

Life is what happens to you while you're busy making other plans.

~*John Lennon*[51]

Management research has demonstrated for quite some time that clearly articulated goals and accountability are important ingredients in business success. But did you know that a rigid attachment to any desired assignment or outcome can actually harm an organization? New research at the Wharton School of Business, conducted after the failure of corporations like Enron and even well-meaning mandates like "No Child Left Behind," suggest that when goal-setting becomes inflexible and unreflective, it creates an environment of tunnel vision, distrust, and dishonesty.[52] Sometimes, you have to recognize that a plan is heading toward a dead end and change course.

Consider the career of singer Natalie Merchant. She had great success with the band Ten Thousand Maniacs in the 1980s; at the start of the 1990s, she felt ready to pursue a solo career. Her first two solo albums performed well, but she really wanted to work with the legendary producer T Bone Burnett. After some preliminary meetings, Burnett told Merchant that he felt she was singing in the wrong vocal range, and strongly urged her to get a vocal coach. At first, she was insulted—she had won Grammy awards! But after some thought, she decided to let go of her own expectations and took his advice. The result was her 2001 album *Motherland*, a Billboard hit and critical success, in which many reviewers complimented the richness and complexity of her voice. Merchant's access to Burnett and her subsequent success was the result of the ability to shift her goals and tactics in the face of new information.

No one can plan or predict everything. Circumstances change, often without warning. If, as Jon Bon Jovi suggests, you map out your plans in pencil, you will always be able to change course and take advantage of new developments.

Celebrate Goals Attained

If you ever visit an established recording studio, you will notice that the walls are lined with gold records. As a matter of fact, so are the walls in rock stars' rec rooms. And if one of them doesn't have a scrapbook full of clippings and positive reviews, you can bet his mom does. Take this as license to celebrate your successes. If the rock stars do it, so can you.

When you meet a goal, send out an e-mail to your band and praise them for a job well done. If you beat a target or win an award, update your fans with the information. This is especially easy to do with social media like Facebook and Twitter. A small victory can be publicized with a quick update at no expense; people will hear the good word, and no one will accuse you of making too much of a minor win.

If a significantly good thing happens, be sure to mention it in your updates, newsletters, events, and even social meetings. Put awards and recognitions on a shelf or wall where visitors can see them. Seriously—don't let them collect dust in a break room. Reward great performance and progress—even your own—with recognition and treats. Something as simple as a catered coffee or small denomination gift card can do a lot to boost morale.

G chord Drill
Your Gold Records

What *are* gold records in your field or market? What forms do recognition and praise take? Ask your band this question. Make a list of the things that constitute a "gold record achievement" according to your vision and goals. When you attain one of those things, announce it and celebrate.

Goals vs. Obsessions

Though I still have no semblance of a life outside of Nine Inch Nails at the moment, I realize my goals have gone from getting a record deal or selling another record to being a better person, more well-rounded, having friends, having a relationship with somebody.

~Trent Reznor[53]

Let's face it. The Nine Inch Nails front man may not be a poster boy for normality, but he raises an important point about rock stardom. Climbing to the top of your profession or calling takes a lot of energy and focus. You have to be disciplined and diligent, make sacrifices, and give it your undivided attention. With that kind of desire and those kinds of high stakes, it is easy for your goals to become obsessions. There is a reason that rock stars get stereotyped as self-absorbed, difficult, and troublesome. When you have an obsession, other things tend to fade into the background, and unfortunately, that often includes people you care about and responsibilities in other areas of your life.

So, you and your band should include reality checks into your goals. That is, make it a goal to be a full spectrum human being, with healthy interpersonal relationships, hobbies, and time to relax. Make time to play, be sure your band is able to maintain personal obligations and make a little fun part of your daily routine. Don't wait until these things seem like a BHAG themselves.

Playing Your G Chord

Let's make this one a chord progression:
Go from B – your band's vision,
To G – the steps to achieve it,
To F – involving your fans,
To G minor (or major) – making adjustments as needed,
To A – keeping everyone's attitude and spirits high.
Get those changes down, and you'll be ready to take on our next chord, and make the big decisions.

Guitar Lesson 4
G Chord

Your goals are an important expression of your band's vision. You need to have clearly articulated goals in order to achieve rock star status.

Things To Remember

1. You can start with a small vision, but aim to develop a BHAG at some point during your band's work.
2. Keep a set list of your best stuff.
3. Get out in the public and play.
4. Celebrate your successes.
5. Include reality checks as part of your regular activities.
6. Your G chord is best played in progression, including your B (band), F (fans), and A (attitude).

D Chord
DECISIONS

It is impossible to get through a day without making decisions. You decide to get out of bed. You decide what to eat for breakfast, and whether to stop for coffee on the way to work. You decide what to wear, whether to call your mom, and if you really need that new mp3 player.

But those are not the decisions we're going to discuss. Your D Chord connects to the big DECISIONS. The tough decisions. The life-changing decisions. Rock stars make them and they make the news. The right choice can mean millions in royalties. The wrong one may result in living out of your van for a while.

Consider Beyoncé Knowles. Her father managed her musical career for much of her professional life. Her music was considered the family business, in a way. And in the industry, they were known to be very close. But in early 2011, her publicist made the announcement that her father and she had ended their "professional relationship." Immediately, the pop culture press started digging for dirt, and reports surfaced that he had mismanaged her funds.

Some records suggested he might have even stolen some money. Beyoncé, her family, and her organization have chosen to keep very quiet about what actually happened—which shows great wisdom and restraint.[54] Nevertheless, you know that it had to be a very difficult and painful time. I think Thanksgiving at their house won't feel the same for many years to come. Imagine what would you do if you were faced with a situation like that? Some day, some way, you just might. Because that's how life works. We all have to make a big, difficult decision at some point.

These are the decisions that breed speculation, alter the course of your life, and generally scare you to death. Some of them are exciting, and leave you breathless with anticipation. Others are just really painful. Each case is different. But one thing remains true: you and your band will be faced with big decisions on your journey, probably more than once. What you choose to do and how you choose to do it will be equal factors in your success.

Chapter 11

DECISIONS

You have an opportunity to be in control of your life for yourself by the decisions that you make.

~ Sean "Puffy" Combs[55]

Your D chord is different from every other chord. You can practice and practice, but until the moment of performance, you won't know exactly what it will sound like. I guess you could say that you don't practice big decisions, you practice for them.

Queen's lead guitarist Brian May was just months away from completing a Ph.D. in Astronomy when the band started gathering steam in 1971. He had invested much of his life in his graduate work and dreamed of becoming an astronomer. Queen was a promising adventure, but a big risk too. How many rock bands actually make it? And if he left his studies, would he ever be able to return? May has said, "It was a tough decision back then to leave my studies for music…but my love for music was stronger." His choice required both faith and sacrifice. He put aside a career to which he had already devoted serious time and effort in order to participate in the band's vision.[56]

May's story does have an uncommonly happy ending. He came back to the thesis after many years, and in 2007 he finished, was awarded a Ph.D., and now divides his time between the university and the recording studio.

Before we get going to the tough stuff, let's remember that decisions can come from positive change. You can trust that some big decisions will be the good and exciting kind. They will be connected to growth, new partnerships, and great opportunities. You should direct most of your mental energy to those instead of burning your mojo on what might go wrong. Your vision and your goals are there to help you take focused action. They will guide you when you see a doorway opening, so listen to what your gut says about whether to walk through, run through, or turn away.

Remember the guitar hero Stevie Ray Vaughan? The band's big break came from an unexpected invitation to play at the Montreux Jazz Festival. It didn't seem like the most obvious fit for his band, Double Trouble, and they were nervous about how they would be received. But the opportunity was thrilling and to Switzerland they went. It was the scene of their big break. Vaughan described the result: "As soon as we were finished, someone came backstage and told us that David Bowie wanted to meet us. We went to the musician's bar at the casino where we talked for hours. We ended up playing at the bar for several nights, and Jackson Browne came in and jammed with us." Seeing and seizing the opportunity launched the band's career—Bowie invited Vaughan to tour with him and play on his next album; Browne helped them produce their first major record.[57]

To make your vision a reality, you and your band have to be ready for these moments, and commit to acting when they arrive. As you set goals, do everything you can to be ready to achieve them when the moment arrives. When it does, go for it!

When The Going Gets Tough
If your time to you
Is worth savin'
Then you better start swimmin'
Or you'll sink like a stone
For the times they are a-changin'.

Bob Dylan, "The Times the are a-Changin"[58]

There is a great story about Joan Jett's first band, the Runaways. Their manager, Kim Fowley, knew that they would be playing in rough clubs for very drunk teenagers. During their rehearsals, he would occasionally surprise them by throwing bottles and cans at their heads until they learned to deal with the unexpected. He wanted them to be prepared, to keep playing, and to react in a way that fit the band's image. Not something that every band would tolerate....but what *do* you do when the audience turns on you?[59]

Should you create contingency plans in preparation for a similar problem in the future? It depends. If the potential problem is one with legal ramifications, or that could threaten the life and health of people connected to your organization, then yes, you should have crisis plans in place. Is the problem one that routinely strikes organizations like yours (such as theft, hacking, equipment damage)? Then take reasonable precautions to minimize the impact of a major loss. A good musical example is the theft of equipment. I can't tell you how many bands have had their amps and instruments stolen from a van. Knowing that to be the case, touring groups can save themselves a lot of potential heartbreak by deciding to invest in good insurance, and setting aside those funds early on. Making that commitment can be tough because resources are often scarce when you are starting out, and it hurts to spend money for something you might never need. But those are the moments when forethought and caution can save your bacon.

Be careful how much of your time and energy you invest on hypothetical risks. A problem may arise more than once, but it may never manifest in the same way twice. If you immerse yourself in what *might* happen, you may miss what is *actually* happening.

What you can and should do, is spend time with your band on creating an effective communication channel. It isn't about asking, "What do we do if things get tough?", but "How should we react when things get tough?" Develop positive and constructive methods of communicating with one another. Make expectations, responsibilities, and chains of command clear. Continually affirm your vision and confirm everyone's ongoing commitment to it.

D Chord Drill
War Stories

Take a moment to think about previous situations in your life that demanded a difficult decision. What was the nature of the problem? Was it financial? Was it interpersonal? Was it logistical? Try to make a list of the "top ten" decisions in your life so far. Ask your band to do the same. Share the stories, including the decision that you made and the outcome that resulted. This will give everyone a common picture of the kinds of obstacles that you may confront.

The guys in Metallica could be the poster children for the consequences of failing to do this. A 2004, documentary film, *Some Kind of Monster*, lays bare the band's toxic relationships and follows them through an intensive therapy process.

I felt the hardest thing for me in the wake of our success was trying to figure out who I was and establishing my own identity, coming to grips with "Who is Lars?" and not just "Who's Lars, the drummer of Metallica?"

~ *Lars Ulrich*[60]

Though they had a huge fan base, multiple best selling records, and *very* fat wallets, their band relationship was full of anger, resentment, and conflict. The film shows two things very clearly: 1) that things were bad enough that the organization could be destroyed by it, and 2) that the members were still committed enough to the vision to try and make it work. Many, many bands would not have survived under these circumstances. Metallica decided to invest serious time and money in a therapy process, one of the members underwent eleven months of rehab treatment, and eventually they settled their differences. The decision required several very angry, wounded people to put the band's needs above their own feelings. But they are still making music.

Of course, not every big decision results in a positive outcome. Ulrich has also confessed that releasing a documentary about the experience was a poor choice; he has said that it made their relationship too public, and has created embarrassment when they meet with their peers in the music industry.[61]

Your band should set forth some guidelines to help you manage tough times with more grace than Metallica. When life gets tough for your band, remember our advice from Chapter 5: get everyone together and determine whether you are dealing with a setback or a problem. Get consensus about the causes and talk about ways to fix it or wait it out.

When there is a major fire to extinguish, crisis management research has a lot of good advice for what to do. According to Professor Timothy Coombs of the Institute for Public Relations, get your communication channels in place early.[62] Make sure all band members, fans, and the public have access to information. Whether you use e-mails, interoffice memos, phone calls, newsletters, or a Twitter stream, make sure people know where to go for accurate information. Designate someone to disseminate information so that you don't have multiple narratives whizzing around.

Second, as Coombs says, "(1) be quick, (2) be accurate, and (3) be consistent." Your internal and external communications should handle and respond to questions and concerns promptly and diligently. Don't withhold information by default; make conscious choices about who needs to know what, and keep your people informed to an appropriate degree.

Third, deal with both the actual problem and with the stress that accompanies it. If your building is hit by a tornado, if your manager dies in a car accident, even if you are faced with a potential hostile take over—whatever the crisis may be, you need to handle practical concerns and manage your band's grief, shock, anxiety, and other emotions.

When Tragedy Strikes

It is very possible that you and your band may experience a catastrophic loss. Someone might die or sustain a terrible injury. A fire could wipe out all of your worldly possessions. The market could crash through shady dealings within your industry and leave everyone in your market with zero business. What do you do when the roof falls in? Def Leppard had an amazing response.

The story is well publicized, and was even dramatized in a TV movie about the band. Def Leppard started the 1980s with a steady stream of success. Their sound got the attention of a top-notch producer; they made two hit albums and became an MTV favorite. The band relocated from England to Ireland and started work on a new record. Then in December 1984, their drummer Rick Allen suffered a major car accident. He lost an arm. But he made the decision while still in the hospital to keep drumming anyway. It might seem absolutely impossible for a one-armed drummer to even exist. But Allen decided to find a way. And the band supported him. They held off recording until he had healed, and rehearsed with him while he worked on a modified drum kit. Two years later, he joined them on tour, with a second drummer to help when he needed it. In the fall of the next year, they released a new album.

You know, people have said to me, 'I don't know what I would have done if I'd have gone through what you went through.' I just turn around and say, 'Well neither did I.' Until you discover that part of yourself, it's inexplicable. You just have to go through the experience, and somehow you're inspired.

~ Rick Allen, Def Leppard[63]

There was never a question of folding up or Rick not being able to do it - it never came up. Through Rick's attitude, we knew that he would pull through.

~ Rick Savage, Def Leppard[64]

That ought to be enough for one group of guys to handle. Unfortunately, lightning struck twice, this time when their lead guitarist died of an accidental overdose in 1991. The band decided to complete the album they had been working on, and committed to staying together. Eventually, they brought a new guitarist into the mix, and have continued to tour and produce new work ever since.

The lesson of Def Leppard is this: when things fall apart, you have two choices. You can break up, or you can hold it together. If your band doesn't make it through a catastrophe, make a goal of parting on friendly, supportive terms. And keep playing your A Chord through the failure. If you determine to tough it out:

- Keep your vision in front of you all the time. Repeat it to one another every day, put it on sticky notes around your house, or print it on t-shirts. But keep your eyes on it.
- Find the patience to put plans on hold indefinitely. Commit to rebuilding what's been lost, whether it is a facility or a key position in your organization.
- Decide what you can live without. Find ways to simplify and strip down your efforts.
- Be generous with each other. Treat one another well, give each other space. Forgive if someone lashes out. You are all struggling.
- Keep rehearsing.

- Keep your fans in the loop.
- And when you're ready, get back out there.

When Paths Diverge

The life of a band is an epic journey; all members invest a great deal of themselves in a vision, work hard and make serious sacrifices to achieve it, and spend a lot of time building relationships with one another. It can be incredibly painful to let that go, but sometimes it is necessary.

Sometimes an individual member decides that her own personal vision is different from the band's, and realizes that it is time to go. Phish's Trey Anastasio is a great example of this. The band's life revolved around constant touring with major stage shows; eventually he realized that he could no longer sustain the pace. And it could not sustain him.

We had a very complex, interconnected group of friendships that in one way was great to be a part of, but had also begun to eat itself alive...I had to get away from it completely to stay healthy. It was so big, it's hard to describe, but with so many employees, and such large overhead, a certain kind of immobility sets in about any decision.
~ Trey Anastasio, Phish[65]

A band may also realize that one or more members no longer fit the band's direction. The process is easier when the member has betrayed the band's vision or taken a destructive turn. Cutting a member who undermines the band's mission or has become unreliable may be uncomfortable, but it is usually the clear and right choice. Replacing the charismatic but difficult David Lee Roth with Sammy Hagar was a controversial move for Van Halen, but the new line up cleared the way for stronger commercial success.

The situation can be more difficult if conflicts are purely personality-based, or if the individual has done nothing wrong.

When the Beatles replaced Pete Best with Ringo Starr, some angry fans would chant for Pete in the middle of shows. After some time, existing fans saw that the new line up worked, and new fans never knew the difference. The Dixie Chicks faced a similar situation with their original singer Laura Lynch; she was the right front person for regional tours, but did not impress Nashville record executives. Asking her to step aside for a more gifted singer, Natalie Maines, the Dixie Chicks quickly signed with a major label and launched a successful tour. Unfortunately, it also created a rift between the old friends that never really healed.

How do you handle the pain of parting ways?
- Come back to the band's vision (and your own) and measure your feelings against it. Is a change good for that vision, or would it just feel good for you?
- Treat each person with dignity. If you have to let someone go, aim to do it gently. This is for the

best even when the individual in question is an unrepentant jerk.

- Keep the dirty laundry in the closet. Make no public statements about the departing member that carry accusations, recriminations, or even criticism about their personal hygiene.
- Re-affirm your commitment to the existing members and acknowledge their contributions.

Use Your Brain *and* Your Gut

Has considering all of these scenarios given you a headache yet? Well, here's a little information pill that might ease the pain: research suggests that you can often trust your gut when making complicated decisions.

Behavioral scientists have conducted a series of experiments to better understand the role that rationality and emotions play in decision-making processes. The results of repeated testing suggests that decisions with a moderate number of factors to consider should be made with careful contemplation. But when the number of factors jumps to 20 or more significant pieces of information, subjects made better decisions when they listened to the initial facts, walked away for a bit, and then listened to their instincts.

For you and your band, this means that you need not agonize over the right thing when you face a tough choice. If you have done your best to create a healthy organization, and you pay attention to all of the available data in your specific circumstances, you should have a strong instinctive feeling about the right choice. It may not be the *easy* path in most situations, but you will know if it is the *right* one. [66]

Playing Your D Chord

"If you choose not to decide, you still have made a choice."

Rush, *"Freewill"*[67]

Big decisions require discipline and sacrifice. They are hard work. It can be very tempting to put them off, or to ask someone else to make them—anything to avoid that pain. But what Rush says about this is true: choosing to avoid a decision is still a kind of choice. And when you take a passive approach, you lose the agency to make your own change. You become reactive rather than active. So when you play your D Chord, play it with conviction.

Guitar Lesson 5
D Chord

You don't practice decisions, you practice for them. The only way to tell if your choice was the right one is to wait and see the results but if you and your band put the right structures in place, you put yourself in the best position for success.

Things to Remember

1. Focus your energies on the positive, exciting decisions that a strong vision and clear goals supply.
2. Prepare for the tough stuff as best you can (buy insurance!). Don't obsess about potentialities, however.
3. Have crisis plans in place for genuine catastrophes.
4. Develop guidelines with your band for managing conflict.
5. When your band falls on hard times, remember to deal with both the practical problems that arise and the human emotional struggles that go with them.
6. Be rational, gather and study the facts. Then go with what your gut tells you.

C Chord
CHANGES

The key to change…is to let go of fear.

~ Roseanne Cash[68]

You can't be conscious and be a grownup without being familiar with the concept of change. Experience shows each of us that every day will be different from the last, and we will have to respond to new variables. Landscapes change. Seasons change. Feelings change. Minds change. People change. If that sounds like the lyrics to a song, it's probably because it's a theme in *hundreds* of them.

In some ways, we long for change. We want to lose weight and get in better shape. We want to find a more satisfying job, or make more money. We want to get along better with people, or get away from the people who make us crazy.

Then again, change can be such a bummer. Your favorite restaurant changes its menu. Your company outsources whole departments to India or Mexico. The kids took the passion between you and your spouse and smothered it in diaper changes and carpools. Why couldn't things have just stayed the same?

What would happen if you allowed yourself to define both change and success by your own ability to remove or overcome your own obstacles? The events of the last decade certainly have lots of people crying "Why couldn't things just stay the same?!" Somewhere in there, we already know why. Change is part of life. What matters is for each of us to try and leverage change, harness it to move ourselves forward.

As a rock star, I have two instincts, I want to have fun, and I want to change the world. I have a chance to do both.

~Bono[69]

The lead singer of U2, a man known for his flamboyant public persona and his commitment to big social causes, is a great example of the right attitude about change. Your C chord is all about taking an active role in the change that affects your life and your band. Believe that you can use your gifts and opportunities to make things better for yourself and others, and you will. When you play your C chord, you enact your own change, as well as responding proactively to the change that life throws your way. Let me put it this way, rock stars don't just survive change, they make it.

Chapter 12

DON'T JUST SURVIVE CHANGE; MAKE IT!

In order to change the world, you have to get your head together first.

~Jimi Hendrix[70]

A whole branch of business management research exists just to try and figure out the best strategies for change. The questions are complicated enough to fry the brain, but change management studies experts have pinpointed a few key features of leaders who do it well: adaptability, problem-solving, interpersonal relations, motivation, and productivity. Let's look at a few rock stars who do these things well, and the lessons we can learn from them.[71]

Turn It Upside Down

Sometimes we are confronted with systems that don't work for us. Or, at least, we don't fit into them. They aren't *made* for our way of doing things. Do you give up because something doesn't "fit", or do you re-design until it fits like a glove?

Jimi Hendrix is an undisputed guitar god. His life and his career were short, but his influence has been huge….whether you consider his guitar work an evolution or revolution, Hendrix was big. And if he hadn't been able to adapt and problem-solve, his career would not have been possible.

You see, Jimi Hendrix was left-handed. Guitars are made and strung for right-handed people. Hendrix had no formal training as a musician. He listened to artists who inspired him, learned their tricks, and tried to emulate their styles. That was tough for someone playing an instrument not built for his body. If you're a lefty and have ever tried to use right-hand scissors, you know what I mean. If you're a righty and want to understand, try slicing an onion with a left-handed knife. Even if you understand the principle, *nothing* works the way that it should. It is like the tool is fighting you. It's surprising he didn't smash more guitars!

Hendrix used a little imagination instead. He rotated his guitar and re-strung it. Basically, he turned his Stratocaster upside down. He still took the trouble to learn the chords (all he had was his guitar, three chords, and the truth, remember?). He still listened and learned from everything his heroes were doing. But he took a limitation and he literally turned it upside down. By the time he arrived in London for his big break, he had developed a sound that stunned Eric Clapton and Jeff Beck. He just needed to find a way to surmount the difficulty of using equipment that was built for someone else...and I'm sure that countless guitarists whom he inspired would say that he managed just fine.

Dream It All Up Again

U2 has an impressive track record in the rock 'n' roll business. They have been playing together for over 30 years. They have 12 studio albums, and have sold almost 200 million records worldwide. They are in the Rock 'n' Roll Hall of Fame. This is a band that has every right to be satisfied with what they have accomplished. The members have collected enough renown and financial success that they could have called it quits at any time during the last 15 years.

After two Grammy awards for "The Joshua Tree," a blockbuster tour, and a successful documentary titled "Rattle and Hum," the band realized that they had exhausted their energy resources. U2 announced at a 1989 concert that they intended to take an extended break and "go away and... just dream it all up again." They took the time away from touring to experiment in the studio. [72]

The band felt injured by some critics' snarky comments about their recent work, and some personal tensions nearly destroyed their efforts at cutting new tracks. But the members of U2 were dedicated to the idea of "dreaming" something new. They might have been set in their ways and tired of old fights, but they were still committed to the vision.

Among fans of the band, this period is a topic of serious discussion. U2 spent several months in the studio, trying unsuccessfully to cut new songs. They argued constantly. It seemed like a break up was imminent, but after several ugly and uncomfortable sessions, they had an epiphany with the song "One." They found a new rhythm and started working on the tracks that would become *Achtung, Baby!*, an album which featured three hit singles.

The band hit another snag in 2001, when their *Pop* album and accompanying tour did not fare so well with critics or the market. They went back to the studio and tried again with *All That You Can't Leave Behind*. Bono announced that U2 was using this album to "reapply for the job of the best band in the world."[73] Did it work? Their next tour had over 2 million concert attendees. So it must have helped.

U2 provides a great model for adaptability, productivity, and interpersonal relations. First and foremost, they did not take the money and run. At both crisis points in the band's life, the individual members had enough money and fame that they could have walked away and lived easy for the rest of their lives. But the vision of what the band could accomplish kept them going. That's something to admire by itself.

U2 faced two major moments of creative drought, but they quickly diagnosed the problem and created space for rest and recreation. Plus, they repeatedly showed public humility and adaptability by acknowledging that they had growing to do. Before both albums, they explored new trends in pop and rock music, and found sources of inspiration for their own work. They learned from the latest information, and committed themselves to building the best product that their combined skills could provide.

And through it all, they remained committed to respecting each other. The members of U2 began their partnership as very young men, and they have remained committed to respecting one another's talents and humanity. In both situations, the individual members recall very angry moments and heated, passionate exchanges. They looked at parting ways, but they never forgot to honor the personal connections between them. That, more than anything else, might be what saved the band. Your group can make a living off of playing golden oldies for the rest of your life (plenty of bands do), but to survive, a mutual respect has to prevail.

Fortunately for U2's fans, their interpersonal skills were just part of the mix. They recognized when stagnation had set in. They created time and space for rest and new ideas. And when they thought their fans were getting impatient, they reaffirmed their public commitment by "reapplying" for the job of their favorite band. In both cases, the band followed a strategy of: 1) acknowledging the need for change, 2) notifying their fans of their intentions, 3) exploring new trends in the market, and 4) working through stress until they returned to consensus. These instincts have allowed U2's members to stay together, stay productive on a professional level, and stay content on a personal one.

Walk This Way

The phrase "walk this way" in its earliest form is actually a vaudeville joke. The American comedy establishment has been working it since the early 1930s. Aerosmith borrowed the phrase as a kind of quintessential line for their 1975 hit of the same title, which narrated the story of a typical American teen's chance to lose his virginity. If parents found the idea tacky, their kids found the song irresistible.

In the mid-1980s, Aerosmith was already a fantastically successful rock group. We have discussed that in other chapters. But at a certain point, their energy had fizzled. Steven Tyler and the other members all needed to consider rehab, and the band was exhausted. They had not had a hit in quite some time.

Then someone introduced their song "Walk this Way" to the budding rap group Run-DMC. It had a great groove, and they might be able to do something new with it. Then a producer suggested maybe Aerosmith could be brought in to collaborate. It was a huge opportunity and risk for both groups. As far as Run-DMC was concerned, rap might sample, but it did not borrow or cover whole songs. And from Aerosmith's perspective, rap had nothing to do with what rock was about or who they were. But it was a great song. And both groups admitted there was potential for something exciting in the proposed collaboration. So, Run-DMC re-worked the lyrics for the new beat, and Aerosmith practiced delivering the melody in a fresh way. They cut a track and released a video. Their collaboration took the rock music world by storm, hitting #4 on the Billboard chart. It accomplished two things at once: 1) affirming the possibilities for rap as a mass-market medium, and 2) introducing a new generation to what Aerosmith had to offer.[74]

Both bands benefitted from the situation. Aerosmith got the chance to enter a new market. The members of the band had to clean up in order to take advantage, so they made that commitment. Run-DMC got to show off their stuff with the support of some very well established rock stars, and the video itself was totally awesome. Who wouldn't appreciate the walls between rap and hard rock being broken down by musicians?

If you consider that, learning to "walk this way" is not so much about imitating the success of past stars. It is about taking the gifts you already possess and applying them to fresh and available materials. One of the beauties of the joint Aerosmith/Run-DMC video was the clear message about collaboration. The musicians removed all obstacles when they heard the call of an irresistible sound.

When Aerosmith and Run-DMC decided to "walk this way" together, both bands had to put aside certain pre-conceived notions in order to imagine the new ground that the collaboration might break. Both groups had the opportunity to use their existing talents, but had to revise their ideas about who they were and what their audience wanted.

C Chord Drill
Innovate or Starve

This is an exercise for a retreat, training, or team-building situation. Get your band access to a kitchen. Give them a recipe and ingredients to make a meal and let them get started. Watch them from an out of the way spot, and step in every 10 minutes to take away some key item. Maybe you take away the butter first, then a mixing bowl, then the person with the best knife skills, then the recipe itself. The band has to find a way of substituting or coping without the things you have removed.

Let them manage the situation on their own. You should only step in if emotions get too charged.

At the end, have everyone sit down to eat what the band has prepared. Over the meal, talk about the experience. How did band members feel when certain things changed? How well do they feel they adapted? Did anyone do something especially well? Anything they wish they had done differently? Break down the processes that were used for different moments of decision. Which methods were successful? Which ones were not?

A completely different (and perhaps bizarre) example of the same impulse created a joint tour between Sammy Hagar and David Lee Roth in 2002. The music world's collective jaw dropped when it was announced. As competing lead singers for Van Halen, these guys have always been happy to show their mutual hatred with acid comments to the press. The only thing they had in common at the time was that they both left Van Halen on bad terms.

Still, they were confident that audiences would pay to hear them sing the Van Halen songs that they had made famous. They titled it the "Sam and Dave" tour, and played multiple U.S. cities, and drew huge crowds as one of the summer's top 10 moneymaking tours. They still couldn't stand each other, but seemed to make their fighting part of the show's publicity: no stage time together, two entirely separate sets, two separate bands, separate modes of travel between gigs, and plenty of quotable insults for the press. They were smart enough to keep the trash talk off stage, and careful to tell interviewers that the other guy might be a jerk, but he put on a great show.[75]

Roth and Hagar had both confronted unwelcome change—being kicked out of a top band in very publicly embarrassing ways—and then turned the situation around in their favor. In a sense, the tour was a way of showing that they could still do Van Halen's songs without Van Halen. They took obvious weaknesses, their ugly rivalry and big egos, and turned them into a publicity strength. They made fans very happy by putting on a great show. As a result, both rock stars were able to regain control of their public images in the wake of being fired, and walked this way... all the way to the bank.

Playing your C Chord

Having a strong C chord is a survival skill, perhaps more than any other single chord in this book. Nurture your own adaptability. Learn to problem-solve by putting yourself in situations where you have to practice that skill. Work on assigning priorities correctly, and then keep your band's focus on the most essential things. If you can't diffuse conflict, then find ways to make it work for you. These are the skills that will help you weather the changes that life throws at you. And they are the tools that help you enact your own change.

A strong C chord will also help get your other chords rockin':

- it boosts your A chord by giving the means to manage failure,
- supports your B chord by enhancing your band's talents,
- and sustains your G chord so you can achieve your goals.

Guitar Lesson 6
C Chord

Rock stars don't just survive change, they make it. When you tackle change, the best strategy involves:

- acknowledging the need for change,
- notifying fans of your intentions,
- exploring new trends in the market, and
- working through stress until your band returns to consensus.

Things to Remember:

1. if a system doesn't fit you, or you don't fit in it, try turning it upside down.
2. When you are burned out, create space for rest and relaxation.
3. For your band to survive, mutual respect must always prevail.
4. Walk this way:
   a. Apply your strengths to the available materials, and to fresh ideas.
   b. Look for ways to turn your weaknesses into strengths.

E Chord
ENERGY

We were put here to do the best we can, and we should take our energy and improve our state of being. I think people have had enough negativity.

~Lenny Kravitz[76]

Do you sing rock 'n' roll in the shower? (C'mon, you *know* you do!) Do you crank the tunes when you're in the car? Have you ever rocked out *Risky Business*-style when you were home alone on a Friday night?

I do. And I'll say it loud and proud! I rock out! I love the way a kickin' drum beat makes me feel, and that rush that comes from hearing a monster guitar lick. Music creates energy. And that's the topic of our final chord, the E Chord: ENERGY.

Before you go thinking, "whoa, that's a little new age-y for my taste, big guy...." Energy only *seems* like an abstract idea because we don't spend a lot of time thinking about it. But it is totally essential for you and your band to understand it. You need it to get you motivated and drive you forward, and you need it to draw people to you. I guarantee you that is true whether we are talking about your career, or your non-profit work, or your relationship with your kids. If you want to be your best at the things you care about, you have to develop strong, positive energy. We want to feel positive energy in our lives. And we want to be near people who put that out.

So where do you get it? How do you sustain it? And how do you communicate that energy with other people to get them to share your vision?

Rock stars are perfect role models for mastering your E chord. Rock stars have energy to spare. They use it to get everyone around them up and moving. When you've been to a great rock concert, you leave it feeling energized and excited. When you play the music at home, it gives you a boost. Whether it's fast paced stuff that makes you want to run a marathon, something sweet and sad that comforts you when you're down, or something chill that helps you relax—they're all varieties of positive energy. Rock stars harness that energy to make the songs you love, create the right sound with the band that plays them, and put on the shows that fans can't wait to experience.

Chapter 13

ENERGIZE!

Energy, in a general sense, refers to strength, vitality, power, and the ability to do work. This applies to everything from mammals to rocket boosters. As far as being a rock star goes, energy means passion, vigor, and enthusiasm. Being enthused about a job or activity makes performing even the most menial of tasks easier and more enjoyable, leading to a better performance. Rock star energy is a well of inspiration and a source of drive. It is also the ability to share that power with others; it's highly infectious, it spreads like wildfire, and it makes amazing things happen.

The Black Eyed Peas put on one of the biggest, most spectacular, you-gotta-get-up-and-move shows in rock music—costumes, laser lights, and a female singer who can do one handed back flips across the stage. The Peas promise their audiences a great time at what amounts to high tech dance party with a very talented and unique group of people. Will.i.am has joked that "You'd find it hard to make up our group… we are more like a mad, worldwide science project than a band."[77] While the dancers and video screens are mind blowing, it is ultimately the group's charismatic performance that audiences come to see. Their name is pretty much synonymous with energy; they even named one

of their albums "The E.N.D", which stands for "the energy never dies." It was for the excitement that their songs and performances generate that the group was invited to play the Super Bowl half time show in 2011. It also gives the band an entrepreneurial vision that allows them to both actively pursue corporate partnerships and to form multiple charity projects. Um, waiter, can we have what they're having?

"If there's any definition of the Peas, it would be freedom. Freedom of all the colors that music does to our lives and participating in that."

~will.i.am, the Black Eyed Peas[78]

Get Your Motor Runnin'

I get the greatest feeling when I'm singing. It's other-worldly. Your feet are anchored into the Earth and into this energy force that comes up through your feet and goes up the top of your head and maybe you're holding hands with the angels or the stars, I have no idea.

~Cyndi Lauper

How do you find the energy to motivate you and your band? Sometimes when you are tapped into it and it flows naturally, energy does seem like the mystical force that Cyndi Lauper describes. That may seem even truer when you can't find it. Rest assured that there are techniques out there to help you find energy in meaningful, reliable ways.

Laser focusing on your vision is a great way to start. A recent management book, *Enlightened Leadership*, suggests that business teams find huge resources of energy when they weigh their activity to focus more on team strengths and opportunities and less on problems and obstacles. The difference is in concentrating on the ideas that move you forward, rather than the ones that hold you back. The book's authors, Oakley and Krug, advise their readers to concentrate on positive questions: "What do we do well? How can we grow? How can we make opportunities to do the things we do well?" As you already know, that's playing your B chord, cultivating your band's vision.[79]

I have my ideas, I have my music, and I also just enjoy showing off, so that's a big part of it. Also, I like to get up onstage and behave insanely or express myself physically, and the band can get pretty silly.

~Bruce Springsteen[80]

The Boss has a 40 year reputation for amazing concerts—epic three hour gigs full of music, stories, and jokes—so he's a great case study for energizing your band. First, Springsteen and E Street look at what they do as a creative exchange. It's about the music and the ideas.

Also, they know how to play their A chords: they have the attitude. The band knows that everyone there is talented, hardworking, and loved by the audience, so they feel free to show off and have some fun. They take the work seriously, but they understand the value enjoying the moment.

Also, Springsteen has a commitment to his physical and mental health. See the guy on stage and you would never imagine that he's over 60 years old. He stays fit and eats well, makes time to rest, and takes time away from performing to recharge. None of us can prevent what time's going to do to us—those joints and that hair will eventually go—but anyone can, and should, take action to stay healthy. You can rock a lot longer if you're not 30 pounds overweight and hunched over a desk for 12 hours a day.

And it was a testament to the life force that I think was at the core of our music - that nobody gave up on you. And that lasted a long time. People got pulled out of a lot of holes. And I would include myself, in different ways over many, many different years.

~Bruce Springsteen[81]

Bands that stay together a long time and stay effective do so because the members offer mutual support. No one is saying that you have to take beach vacations and spend Christmas together. But your band members should speak and act with as much warmth and respect as you can muster. Watch for signs of struggle from individual team members and offer support. Don't skimp on praise or encouragement—everyone should feel empowered to tell a band mate "Good job!" You should also get involved in the wider world as a group. Organize a softball game for fun, or get everyone together for a charity walk. You need to do at least a little bonding to allow positive feelings to grow - get people invested in one another.

As the bandleader, it is up to you to feed everyone's commitment to the vision, get everyone working every day to hone your chops, and write songs you believe in.

Head Out on the Highway

... I assume people come for the very same reasons as they do when I'm with the band: to be moved, for something to happen to them.

~Bruce Springsteen[82]

When your band's sound and energy is right, you'll have what you need to energize fans. The strength of your product and your confidence in each other will translate into high power enthusiasm. Your joy in doing something well will make it a pleasure to perform. That enthusiasm can be infectious, but only to people who come into direct contact with it. To play your E chord, you need to get your show on the road and connect with them.

Once you get that two-way energy thing going, everyone benefits hugely.

~James Taylor[63]

First, is your E chord in tune? Have you done the research to figure out who your audience is, identified where you will find them, and gotten to know them? Then you will be ready to play their song.

The most basic rule of engagement is that you bring the love you want to receive. That means eye contact, it means smiling and engaging, and asking questions. You don't have to pretend to be someone you are not, but you do have to be in a good mood and glad to be there. Everyone wants to be wanted. If you walk into a room full of people, demand their attention, and then behave as though you'd rather be somewhere else, you'll lose them so fast your nose hair will burn. But if you express appreciation and admiration, people will open up to you.

If you are having an off day and the excitement isn't there, fan the flames of your own enthusiasm by focusing on your very favorite parts of what you do. Once you get your fans engaged, that two-way energy James Taylor talks about will kick in. The fans will get excited, and that will give you the boost you need to get through the gig with style.

Fans love to be asked for their participation in your work. Their efforts are a source of energy for you, and their enthusiasm can recharge your band when they're feeling spent. This is an especially useful technique when you have an event coming up. Acts as diverse as Steely Dan and David Gray have started crowdsourcing their set lists, inviting fans to vote for songs online before concerts. Think about the possibilities for building anticipation and excitement before the doors even open.

Another great way to harness your fans' energy is to throw them a party. In other words, create an unusual and festive event for them. Remember back in Chapter 9 we talked about Amanda Palmer's impromptu online gathering with her Twitter followers? What would you call that if not a "surprise party"? A number of big bands are starting to work on uncommon events for their fans. KISS, Weezer, Jerry Jeff Walker, and other stars have sponsored cruises for their audiences. These include all of the typical tropical perks of a cruise (ridiculous amounts of food, beaches, and sunshine) plus multiple performances and opportunities to meet and interact with the performers. Between the novelty of seeing your favorite band at sea, the promises of close contact, and the fun they already associate with cruises, fans are happy to pay the premium prices that bands charge. Promise them something fun, something new, and a chance to get close to you, and watch the enthusiasm you will generate![84]

Lookin' for Adventure
Yesterday has come and gone
and I've learned how to leave it where it is
and I see that I was wrong
for ever doubting I could win…
I will break these chains that bind me,
happiness will find me

leave the past behind me,
today my life begins
a whole new world is waiting
it's mine for the taking
I know I can make it,
today my life begins
                    ~Bruno Mars, "Today My Life Begins"[85]

Your energy can be a big factor in determining your access to opportunity. Psychologist Barbara Frederickson conducted an extended study on the affects of positivity in a person's life over time. She found that your individual positive emotions will come and go (duh, they're called *moods*), but that people who felt more positive emotions and felt them more often were also more creative, resilient, and successful.[86]

The presence of positive, enthusiastic energy affects whether you see the openings that might be right in front of you, and whether you have the confidence to take them. If you and your band commit to Bruno Mars's mantra ("today our lives begin"), you will be on the lookout for anything that makes it happen.

Energy can also influence whether people will take a chance on you. Why should they give you something you want if you don't project confidence? Your swagger is an expression of positive energy. Plus, people are more likely to go out of their way for you if they like you. So remember to treat potential collaborators well.

Practice your E Chord
Jam to <u>Your</u> Rock Stars

Behavioral research shows that songs with positive lyrics make people more upbeat and considerate. They actually treat each other better. You and your band should pick a play list of your favorite positive songs. These should be the *real* gut-grabbers, the ones you can't help but move and sing along with. Keep these songs handy on your computer, sound system, or MP3 player. Everyone in the band should have a copy. When your energy is lagging or you're discouraged, turn it on and turn it up! You can do this when you are alone, or when you are together.

And when you do get the music started, get up and move. Yes, even if you feel like a dork. Just let go, get up, and dance like a maniac. Sing into a Sharpie pen. You'll feel better in five minutes, and you'll be better company too.

Whatever comes your way
We are the product of our on environment repent
With equality, plus duality
And taken all kind of possibilities
I sing the song from the soul
Let it rise from the tone
Let it rhythmically grow
Into its own life
Let it become you
Then you become it
                    ~The Black Eyed Peas, "Positivity"[87]

Energy is a driving factor in how you manage change, too. It makes sense. I have talked about how closely connected opportunity and change are. The mindset and strategies you need are the same in both cases.

You can't find a better case study for committed, survivor, rock star energy than the band INXS. In 1997, their lead singer Michael Hutchence died unexpectedly. His band mates, all close friends, were heartbroken. They took some time off, but soon came back together. They still believed in the band's vision. Most bands don't survive when their front man dies; INXS wanted to beat the odds.

It took them a long time to remake themselves, a very long time. For a decade, they performed gigs with other singers substituting for Hutchence. Many well-known rock stars pitched in from time to time, but they couldn't find the right fit. Finally, they decided on an unprecedented step. And if you are a fan of reality TV, you might already know what it was.

We likened it to going into the dentist's chair. You know it's going to hurt, but you'll come out with much better teeth.
~ Andrew Ferriss, INXS[88]

INXS partnered with CBS television on a reality show called "Rock Star" to seek a new lead singer. Hopeful rockers from all over auditioned for the TV studio, who picked 15 finalists. Over the course of several weeks, the band worked with each of the finalists and participated in a series of challenges meant to test the contestant's skills. At the end of the show, the band chose a winner (with some help from TV audiences and CBS, of course) and set out on a tour. Their relationship with the new guy, J.D. Fortune, was not as easy as with their old friend, and he left the band after two years. But the experiment got INXS back into the public eye, reenergized them, and gave them hope that they could carry on.[89]

The lesson here is that all of the members of INXS had difficult, painful times after they lost their band mate. They felt lost. They doubted themselves. But they came back to the vision of the band. They kept trying and kept experimenting, and kept moving forward when an idea did not work. They worked through the change that life threw at them and went on to create their own change. And if recent press on the band is any indication, the world thinks they deserve to be rock stars for that alone.

Playing Your E Chord

Your E chord is an amazing tool. You can play it with any of your other chords, and you can play it with all of them at once. Get your energy tuned first; decide with your band what steps you need to take to find inspiration, stay motivated, and act positive. Then play your other chords. The band energy will go a long way to winning fans and to keeping them loyal. Then you can work on mobilizing their energy, which will push your vision forward and help sustain you in times of need.

Guitar Lesson 7
E Chord

Rock Star Energy is positive. It is a source of inspiration and drive. It fuels your band and draws in fans.

Things to Remember:

1. Energy comes from having a vision you believe in.
2. Energy is sustained by caring for your physical and mental health.
3. Energy is restored through mutual support between yourself and your band, your band and your fans.
4. Bring the love/energy you want to receive with you into your interactions with others.
5. Energize your fans by asking them to participate in your work.
6. People who stay positive over the long term tend to see and seize more opportunities than those who tend toward pessimism or fatalism.
7. Opportunity and change are connected. Your state of mind will determine whether you have the energy you need to manage them.

Afterword

And that's all, folks. Now you have seven chords and the truth. It's time to go out and do what the legends did when they were all rock-stars-in-training. You need to get your instruments, get the band together, and play.

It is okay to start with a small vision, and with simple songs. But stretch yourself, and engage your imagination. If you aren't ready for a BHAG yet, you will be.

Practice your chords every day. Find a way to bring them into your life a little at a time. Start with those three basic chords, and take some small action—promise yourself that you will do *something* before you go to bed each night. Bring your A chord with you into the conference room or the PTA meeting, and be just a little more assertive about your opinion. Play it when you're disappointed that something fell through and let it inspire you to try again. Run those B chord drills when you're frustrated and angry with the people around you, or when you have to inspire everyone to stay late and work on that tight sound. Get a LinkedIn or Twitter account and just try a few simple posts; soon you'll have your F chord down. You can play the songs your fans want to hear, and gather a flock of supporters to help you scale your efforts and get your songs out there.

When those three chords are in tune, your music will come together. You will be ready to set goals, make decisions, face change, and build energy around yourself. Remember those chords add color and depth to every thing you do, so don't neglect them. You may have moments where you feel lost, lose the beat, or lack inspiration. But keep telling yourself and your band to stay focused on your vision. Be willing to experiment, take risks, and fail. One Hit Wonders write the same thing over and over. Rock stars reinvent themselves.

You have the power, the energy, and the knowledge to be a star. Seize the opportunity…and Rock On!

Resources

(Endnotes)

Introduction

[1] "Interview with Steve Jobs." (2008, December 12). *60 Minutes.* Retrieved October 20, 2011, from http://cnettv.cnet.com/60-minutes-steve-jobs/9742-1_53-50004696.html

A Chord - Introduction

[2] "Jerry Garcia Quotes." Retrieved October 16, 2011, from http://www.great-quotes.com/quotes/author/Jerry/Garcia

[3] DeRogatis, J. (2000). *Let it blurt: the life and times of Lester Bangs, America's greatest rock critic.* New York: Broadway Books.

Chapter 1 - Failure

[4] Grigoriadis, V. (2010, March 28) "Growing up Gaga." *New York Magazine.* Retrieved October 15, 2011, from http://nymag.com/arts/popmusic/features/65127/

[5] "Factoids: How many people in the U.S. play musical Instruments." Retrieved October 15, 2011, from http://www.bolzcenter.org/factoids/000065.php

[6] Noble, C. (2011, March 7). "Why Companies Fail—and How their Founders Can Bounce Back." *Working Knowledge The Thinking that Leads.* http://hbswk.hbs.edu/item/6591.html

[7] "Interview: Johnny Cash, country music legend." (1993, June 25). *Academy of Achievement.* Retrieved October 15, 2011, from http://www.achievement.org/autodoc/printmember/cas0int-1

[8] Bon Jovi, J. (2001, May 16). "Monmouth University Commencement Address." Retrieved October 15, 2011, from http://bluehawk. monmouth.edu/~opa/commencement/jbjSpeech.html

[9] Sambora, R. (2004, May 6). "Kean University Commencement Address." Retrieved October 15, 2011, from http://webspace. webring.com/people/da/abb_vetkid/Kean_Univ_RS.html

[10] Noble, C. (2011, March 7). "Why Companies Fail—and How their Founders Can Bounce Back." Working Knowledge The Thinking that Leads. http://hbswk.hbs.edu/item/6591.html

[11] Raitt, B. (1992, May). "Berklee School of Music Commencement Speech." Retrieved October 15, from http://www.berklee.edu/ commencement/past/raitt.html

[12] Aguilera, C. & Storch, S. (2002). "Fighter. United States: Carsters-BMG Music Publishing.

Chapter 2 - Opportunity

[13] Leung, Rebecca. (2009, February 18). "Choosing Music over Religion." CBS.Com. Retrieved October 15, 2011, from http://www. cbsnews.com/stories/2005/02/08/60II/main672415.shtml

Chapter 3 - Yourself

[14] "10 Questions for Will.i.am." (2009, January 8). Time Magazine Arts Blog. Retrieved October 18, 2011, from http://www.time.com/time/magazine/article/0,9171,1870496,00. html#ixzz1bAVXblig

[15] Hiatt, B. (2009, June 11). "Lady Gaga, New York Doll." Rolling Stone. Retrieved October 18, 2011, from http://www.rollingstone. com/music/news/lady-gaga-new-york-doll-rolling-stones-2009-cover-story-20090611

[16] Weisul, Kimberly (2011, Septermber 21). Study: better to be confident than right." BNET.com. Retrieved October 18, 2011, from http://www.bnet.com/blog/business-research/study-better-to-be-confident-than-right/2259?tag=mantle_skin;content

[17] Sawyers, J.S. (Ed.) (2004). *Racing in the Street: The Bruce Springsteen Reader*. New York: Penguin.

[18] Jessica Stillman. (2011, August 11). "How to conquer 'Imposter Syndrome'" Bnet.com. Retrieved October 18, 2011, from http://www.bnet.com/blog/entry-level/how-to-conquer-imposter-syndrome/5343?tag=mantle_skin;content

B Chord - Introduction

[19] Jerome, J. (1976, August 9). "Aerosmith's heavy metal has made Steve Tyler America's hottest home-grown rocker." *Parade* 6.6. Retrieved October 19, 2011, from http://www.people.com/people/archive/article/0,,20066760,00.html

[20] Aerosmith and Davis, S. (2003). *Walk this way: the autobiography of Aerosmith*. New York: Harper Collins.

[21] For an in-depth analysis of KISS's branding strategy, see Blackwell, R. & Stepan, T. (2004). *Brands that rock: what business leaders can learn from the world of rock and roll.*" New York: Wiley.

[22] DeCurtis, A. (n.d.) "Not a businessman...a business, man." *Men's Health Celebrity Fitness Blog*. Retrieved October 19, 2011, from http://www.menshealth.com/celebrity-fitness/not-a-business-man.

Chapter 6 - The Long-Term

[23] Stillman, J. (2011, June 15) "Three things You Don't Understand about Teamwork." BNET.com http://www.bnet.com/blog/entry-level/3-things-you-dont-understand-about-teamwork/4908?tag=mantle_skin;content

[24] Bokris, V. (2003). *Keith Richards: the biography*. Cambridge, MA: Da Capo.

Chapter 6 - Take Charge of Change

[25] Drucker, P. (1999) *Management challenges for the 21st Century*. New York: Harper Collins.

26 Åkerlund, J. & Gonzales, D. (2005). *I'm going to tell you a secret.* [Motion Picture]. United States: Maverick Productions

27 O'Malley Greenburg, Z. (2011, January 12). "Why Lady Gaga will earn $100 million in 2011." Forbes.com. Retrieved October 19, 2011, from http://www.forbes.com/sites/zackomalleygreenburg/2011/01/12/why-lady-gaga-will-earn-100-million-in-2011/

28 Carroll, J. (2001, January 14). "Madonna made in Britain." *Elle.* Retrieved October 18, 2011, from http://allaboutmadonna.com/madonna-interviews-articles/elle-february-2001

29 Grigoriadis, V. (2010, March 28) "Growing up Gaga." *New York Magazine.* Retrieved October 15, 2011, from http://nymag.com/arts/popmusic/features/65127/

30 Baron, R.A. & Ward, T. (2004, Winter) "Expanding Entrepreneurial Cognition's Toolbox: Potential Contributions from the Field of Cognitive Science." <u>Entrepreneurship Theory and Practice</u>. 553-573.

F Chord Introduction

31 "Johnny Depp: My fans are my employer." (n.d.) Fox All Access. Retrieved October 21, 2011, from http://foxallaccess.blogs.fox.com/2011/05/15/johnny-depp-my-fans-are-my-employer/

Chapter 7 - Find Your Fans

32 Sawyers, J.S. (Ed.) (2004). *Racing in the Street: The Bruce Springsteen Reader.* New York: Penguin

33 Nissim, B. (n.d.) "Brand Loyalty: The psychology of preference." Retrieved October 20, 2011, from http://www.brandchannel.com/papers_review.asp?sp_id=680

34 Ibid.

35 Waddell, R. (2011, August 12). "Chris Martin Q&A: 'I always feel like each record is our last.'" *Billboard.* Retrieved October 19, 2011, from

http://www.billboard.com/news/chris-martin-q-a-i-always-feel-like-each-1005314262.story?page=2#/news/chris-martin-q-a-i-always-feel-like-each-1005314262.story?page=2

[36] Scott, D.M. (2009, July 29). "How Amanda Palmer made $11,000 on Twitter in two hours." WebInkNow.com. Retrieved October 19, 2011, from http://www.webinknow.com/2009/07/yesterday-i-enjoyed-spending-some-time-with-amanda-palmer-lead-singer-of-the-dresden-dolls-and-punk-cabaret-force-of-nature.html

Chapter 8 - Keep Your Fans

[37] Anderson, S.E. (2003). *The quotable musician: from Bach to Tupac.* New York: Allworth.

[38] Cohen, S. (1989, March) "Kiss this." *Spin.* 50-51, 80

[39] Calloway, S. (2007). "Sean "Puffy" Combs speaks." MTV.com. Retrieved October 20, 2011, from http://www.mtv.com/bands/archive/p/puffy01_2/index2.jhtml

[40] "About Me." (n.d.) TaySwift Fansite. Retrieved October 21, 2011, from http://www.myspace.com/tayswiftfansite

[41] "Exclusive Interview with Chris Martin." (2003, November 3). *Coldplay E-Zine.* Retrieved October 21, 2011, from http://coldplaynet.tumblr.com/

Chapter 9 -Mobilize Your Fans

[42] Scott, D.M. (2009, July 29). "How Amanda Palmer made $11,000 on Twitter in two hours." WebInkNow.com. Retrieved October 19, 2011, from http://www.webinknow.com/2009/07/yesterday-i-enjoyed-spending-some-time-with-amanda-palmer-lead-singer-of-the-dresden-dolls-and-punk-cabaret-force-of-nature.html

G Chord - Introduction

[43] Petty, T. and Lynne, J. (1991). "Into the Great Wide Open. Warner/Chappell Music, EMI Music Publishing.

Chapter 10 - Go for the Goals

44 Anderson, S.E. (2003). *The quotable musician: from Bach to Tupac.* New York: Allworth.

45 *Famous Quotes & Authors* http://www.famousquotesandauthors. com/authors/madonna_quotes.html

46 Tyler, S. (1973). "Dream On." United States: Columbia Records.

47 Mikal Gilmore (2011, March 3) "The Fury and the Power of the Clash" *Rolling Stone.*

48 "Donny Osmond Quotes". *World of Quotes.* Retrieved Octoer 23, 2011, from http://www.worldofquotes.com/author/Donny+Osmond/1/ index.html.

49 "Q&A: Alicia Keys" (2005, February 10). Alicia Keys Fan Site. Retrieved October 23, 2011, from http://www.aliciakeysfan.com/page/47/

50 Bon Jovi, J. (2001, May 16). "Monmouth University Commencement Address." Retrieved October 15, 2011, from http://bluehawk. monmouth.edu/~opa/commencement/jbjSpeech.html

51 Anderson, S.E. (2003). *The quotable musician: from Bach to Tupac.* New York: Allworth.

52 "Why goal-setting can lead to disaster" (2009, February 19). Forbes.com. Retrieved October 23, 2011, from http://www. forbes.com/2009/02/19/setting-goals-wharton-entrepreneurs-management_wharton.html.

53 Hilburn, Robert. (1999, September). "Further up the spiral." *Los Angeles Times.* Retrieved October 23, 2011, from http://www. theninhotline.net/archives/articles/xart226.shtml

D Chord - Introduction

54 Sean Michaels. "Beyoncé's father alleged to have stolen from her." *Guardian.co.uk* (July 13, 2011) http://www.guardian.co.uk/ music/2011/jul/13/beyonce-father-mathew-knowles

Chapter 11 - Decisions

55   Calloway, S. (2007). "Sean "Puffy" Combs speaks." MTV.com. Retrieved October 20, 2011, from http://www.mtv.com/bands/archive/p/puffy01_2/index2.jhtml

56   "Queen star hands in science PhD." BBC.com. August 3, 2007. http://news.bbc.co.uk/2/hi/6929290.stm

57   Frank Joseph. "Before the flood." *Guitar World.* September 1982. http://www.tangledupinblues.com/beforetheflood.html

58   Dylan, B. (1964). "The times they are a'changin'." United States: Columbia Records.

59   Martins, T. (2010, March 10). "Kim Fowley on "The Runaways' Film: 'Every movie needs a villain, and I'm a good one.'" Los Angeles Times.com. Retrieved October 23, 2011, from http://latimesblogs.latimes.com/music_blog/2010/03/kim-fowley-on-the-runaways-movie-every-movie-needs-a-villain-and-im-a-good-one.html

       Newman, M. (2010, January 26). "Where Does the Film Get it Wrong?" Hitfix.com. Retrieved October 23, 2011, from http://www.hitfix.com/blogs/the-beat-goes-on/posts/cherie-currie-sets-the-record-straight-on-the-runaways

60   Andrew Billen. (2005, March 29). "The Head-banger and the therapist-Rock n Roll!" *The Times London.*

61   "Ulrich: We were Stupid to Make *Some Kind of Monster.*"(2010, July 6). *World Entertainment News Network.*

62   Coombs, T.W. (2007, October 30). *"Crisis Management And Communications.* Institute for Public Relations.com. Retrieved October 24, 2011, from http://www.instituteforpr.org/topics/crisis-management-and-communications/

63   "Rick Allen Quotes". (n.d.) My Def Leppard Fan site. Retrieved October 24, 2011, from http://www.mydefleppard.com/rickquotes.html

64   Ibid.

[65] Blagg, C. (2005, November 15). "Phish story; Anastasio talks about band's breakup, need to `Shine' solo." *The Boston Herald.*

[66] Lehrer, J. (2011, September 20). "How should we make hard decisions?" Wired.com. Retrieved October 24, 2011, from http://www.wired.com/wiredscience/2011/09/how-should-we-make-hard-decisions/

Stillman, J. (2011, September 16). "The scientific case for going with your gut." BNET.com, Retrieved October 24, 2011, from http://www.bnet.com/blog/entry-level/the-scientific-case-for-going-with-your-gut/5533?tag=mantle_skin;content

[67] Lee, G., Lifeson, A. & Peart, N. (1980) Canada: Mercury Records.

C Chord - Introduction

[68] "Rosanne Cash Quotes." *World of Quotes.* Retrieved October 24, 2011, from http://www.worldofquotes.com/author/Rosanne+Cash/1/index.html.

[69] Tyrangiel, J. (2002, March 4). "Bono's Mission." Time.com Retrieved October 24, 2011, from http://www.time.com/time/magazine/article/0,9171,212721-1,00.html

Chapter 12 - Don't Just Survive Change; Make It!

[70] Hewett, M. (2011, September 22). "Remembering Jimi Henrix, warrior poet." *Guitar World.* Retrieved October 24, 2011, from http://www.guitarworld.com/remembering-jimi-hendrix-warrior-poet.

[71] Pagon, M., Banutai, E. and Bizjak, U. (2008, June). "Study report: leadership competencies for successful change management." Slovenia: University of Maribor.

[72] U2 (2006) *U2 by U2.* Neil McCormick, Ed. London: HarperCollins.

[73] Ibid.

[74] For an analysis of this collaboration from a branding perspective, see Blackwell, R. & Stepan, T. (2004). *Brands that rock: what business leaders can learn from the world of rock and roll."* New York: Wiley.

[75] Brown, M. (2002, June 18). "Van Who? Hagar, Roth share the driving on hard-rocking tour." *Rocky Mountain News*.

"Feuding duo takes anger, music on tour; Ex- Van Halen pair comes kicking, screaming to Nissan." (2002, August 10). *The Washington Times*.

Rodman, S. (2002, Aug. 2). "Sammy Hagar pulls no punches on 'Heavyweight' partner David Lee Roth" *The Boston Herald*.

E Chord - Introduction

[76] Pepper, T. (1998). "Lenny's 5." *Deep Joy*. Retrieved October 25, 2011, from http://www.lennykravitz.com/interviewdeepjoy.html

Chapter 13 - Energy

[77] "The good life - the future of rock 'n' roll." (2011, August 3). <u>The Independent</u>.

[78] Ibid.

[79] Mitchell, P. (2011, October 4). "Out in Front: What You Focus on is What You Get." Bnet.com. Retrieved October 25, 2011, from http://www.bnet.com/videos/out-in-front-what-you-focus-on-you-get/6309166?tag=mantle_skin;content

[80] Hagin, M. (2009, January 18). "Meet the new boss" *The Observer*.

[81] Ibid.

[82] Hornby, N. (2005, 16 July). "A fan's eye view: Nick Hornby talks to Bruce Springsteen." *Observer Music Monthly*. Retrieved October 25, 2011, from http://www.guardian.co.uk/music/2005/jul/17/popandrock.springsteen

[83] "James Taylor Quotations" (n.d.) Retrieved October 26, 2011, from http://www.quotations.net/author-quotes/14072/James%20Taylor

[84] Thompson, S.T. (2011, July 21). "Music to Your Ears: 8 Great Rock-and-Roll Theme Cruises." *Cruise News*. Retrieved October 26, 2011, from http://www.cruisecritic.com/news/news.cfm?ID=4554

85 Mars, B. (2010). "Today my life begins." United States: Electra/ Anthem.

86 Frederickson, B.L. (2009). *Positivity: Groundbreaking Research Reveals How to Embrace the Hidden Strength of Positive Emotions, Overcome Negativity, and Thrive.* United States: Crown.

87 Adams, W, Feyen, K, Fratantuno, M, Gomez, J, Lapin, B & Pineda A. (1998) "Positivity". United States: Jeepney Music Publishing, Nawasha Networks Publishing, Will.i.am. Music Inc.

88 "And the band played on: INXS and life after" (2006, August 27). *Canberra Times*.

89 Cornwell, J. (2006, Sept. 21). "A new sensation, again Australian band INXS, silenced by the death of their frontman Michael Hutchence, have been reborn - with a singer found on reality TV" *Daily Telegraph.*

Made in the USA
Columbia, SC
15 June 2022